perennial gardens

Better Homes and Gardens®

perennial gardens

written by Eleanore Lewis

Better Homes and Gardens® Books
Des Moines, Iowa

Better Homes and Gardens® Books
An imprint of Meredith® Books

Perennial Gardens
Project Editor: Cathy Wilkinson Barash
Writer: Eleanore Lewis
Art Director: Lyne Neymeyer
Copy Chief: Catherine Hamrick
Copy and Production Editor: Terri Fredrickson
Contributing Graphic Designer: Beth Ann Edwards
Contributing Copy Editor: Barbara Feller Roth
Contributing Proofreaders: Ellen Bingham, Maria Duryee,
   Alison Glascock, Margaret Smith
Contributing Photographers: Derek Fell, Saba S. Tien
Researcher: Rosemary Kautzky
Indexer: Jana Finnegan
Electronic Production Coordinator: Paula Forest
Editorial and Design Assistants: Kaye Chabot,
   Mary Lee Gavin, Karen Schirm

Meredith® Books
Editor in Chief: James D. Blume
Design Director: Matt Strelecki
Managing Editor: Gregory H. Kayko

Director, Retail Sales and Marketing: Terry Unsworth
Director, Sales, Special Markets: Rita McMullen
Director, Sales, Premiums: Michael A. Peterson
Director, Sales, Retail: Tom Wierzbicki
Director, Sales, Home & Garden Centers: Ray Wolf
Director, Book Marketing: Brad Elmitt
Director, Operations: George A. Susral
Director, Production: Douglas M. Johnston

Vice President, General Manager: Jamie L. Martin

Better Homes and Gardens® Magazine
Editor in Chief: Jean LemMon
Executive Garden Editor: Mark Kane

Meredith Publishing Group
President, Publishing Group: Christopher M. Little
Vice President, Finance & Administration: Max Runciman

Meredith Corporation
Chairman and Chief Executive Officer: William T. Kerr

Chairman of the Executive Committee: E. T. Meredith III

All of us at Better Homes and Gardens® Books are dedicated
to providing you with information and ideas to enhance
your home and garden. We welcome your comments and
suggestions. Write to us at: Better Homes and Gardens Books,
Garden Editorial Department, 1716 Locust St., Des Moines,
IA 50309-3023.

If you would like to purchase any of our books, check
wherever quality books are sold. Visit our website at
bhg.com or bhgbooks.com.

introduction **6**

Before you jump eagerly into planning and designing your perennial gardens, take time to delight in a few ideas for creating the best arrangements. These pages provide a brief overview of some of the elements—color, plant habit, height—that make a successful garden beautiful and ever-changing.

introduction

perennial versatility

Before you begin selecting plants in your favorite colors, take a close look at your yard and discover the range of perennials you can use. Find out the amount and type of sun an intended garden receives; you'll find a range of lovely perennials for shade or light shade in addition to the beautiful ones for full sun. Consider how and when you spend your leisure time; you can find low-maintenance plants, flowers that glow in the evening, and plants that attract butterflies and birds. Think about your entire yard. Look for tall plants to set beside fences, short spreading plants to place along a path or in spaces between stepping-stones, and vining perennials to cover an arbor.

One of the best characteristics of perennials is that you don't need to replant them every year as you do annuals. You might dig and divide them every few years, but you can skip the yearly task that annuals require, giving you more time to enjoy the garden you've designed!

color

Colors are irresistible, even a lush cottage-style garden has a planned exuberance. To get the most out of the shorter bloom time of most perennials, select yours so plants bloom successively from spring through fall.

Remember some of the basics of color. Blues and violets are cool colors; they tend to recede in a garden. Reds, yellows, and oranges are hot; they "pop" in a border. Silver, white, and green—from pale to chartreuse to dark, and every hue in between—are neutral; they help harmonize groups of contrasting colors.

Combining colors well is a relatively easy art to master. Begin with shades of a main color—blue, violet, lavender, purple—add a few clumps of a contrasting yellow or red, and intersperse white flowers or silvery foliage.

color harmony
above: **Tone down bright colors—yellow, orange, and red—with touches of white and silver to keep them from overwhelming your garden design.**

texture
right: **Combine plants that have different foliage and flower textures to add interest to the garden, as these feathery plumes of astilbe and narrow spikes of veronica do.**

sunny splash

above left: Bold colors and sunny locations go together. Appropriate in any season, they are especially welcome in fall when skies seem bluer and trees are beginning to shed their multicolored leaves.

shady palette

left: Spring is the dominant season for gardens in shade. Flower colors may be fleeting, so depend on plants with boldly textured and variegated leaves, like these hostas, to light up the area through summer and fall.

color contrast

above: Blue, red, and yellow are contrasting colors. Their primary hues bring vibrant excitement to a garden. Use shades or tints of the primary colors—lavender and rose, for example—to create a subtle, equally attractive design.

introduction

sizing things up

Tall plants are magnificent. Because they usually spread somewhat in relation to their height, they can fill a garden quickly, making it look lush and mature much faster than if you planted mostly lower-growing perennials. You do, however, need to use them wisely, as a backdrop, an enclosure, or a screen for the entire garden bed.

Midheight perennials are the mainstay of a garden—partly because there are so many of them. Remember that medium-size plants grow between 2 and 4 feet. If you have a small garden or yard, you may want to use the taller of these perennials as your backdrop, rather than go for 5- to 6-foot plants, to keep the bed in scale with the rest of the yard.

Low-growing perennials can play many roles in the landscape. They are perfect for edging a bed or border and make wonderful container plantings. If the plants are spreading types (such as creeping phlox and thyme), you can use them as groundcovers, as decorative accents in a dry stone wall, or to soften the hard edges of a retaining wall as they spill over the top.

When you design a garden, don't be too rigid about heights. Place a couple of midheight perennials toward the front of the bed. Perhaps set a tall plant at the side. The garden will look much more natural and "uncomposed" if you intermingle plant heights a bit. Nature, of course, may do that for you. Plants that readily reseed themselves, such as columbine, corydalis, and knautia, are not particular about where their seeds drop and germinate, so you will always find surprises in the border the following spring. Take advantage of them.

tall specimens

right: Borrow a practice from the English and use perennials, such as crambe and ornamental grasses, not only in a border but also as specimen plants or in a mixed bed with shrubs. In a bed or border, set plants that grow 5 to 6 feet tall at the rear where they will form an imposing backdrop for midheight and shorter plants, such as beebalm and coreopsis.

ground covering

above: Plants that cover the ground quickly and thickly keep weeds from germinating, help prevent soil erosion on slopes, and create a carpet—a living mulch—in shady or sunny areas. If, like thyme, they also flower beautifully, they provide a delightful bonus.

habit forming

The way a plant grows influences how you will use it. Obvious? Not always. You can take advantage of the growth habit of some plants in not-so-obvious ways. Flowers with lax stems, such as red buttons, will stand upright if you support them. Left to their own devices, they also will float or weave attractively among other, sturdier plants. Vines, such as the clematis below, usually climb, but they can also drape—effectively covering a retaining wall or spreading out as a groundcover among upright perennials.

Growth habit often enters into your design in your choices of tall, midheight, and short plants and of naturally bushy, vertical, and spiky plants. To create an interesting planting, combine groups of plants with different growth habits.

low spreading

above: Many low-growing plants, such as creeping phlox and dianthus, spread slowly enough that you can use them as edging plants in a border. Their foliage, often evergreen, stays attractive for months.

climbing high

left: A perennial vine like clematis can wind its way up a trellis, clamber over an arbor, camouflage a fence, or tumble across a stone wall. Flowers add to the beauty, but the shape, color, and texture of the foliage is most important for an all-season design.

perennial gardens | **9**

introduction

looking closely

Gardening is more than planning and planting. The day-to-day joy is in the details, the closeup beauty, and, yes, the little miracles. Watching perennials appear above ground every spring, noticing the shape of a flower, burying your nose into a fragrant peony or lily, spotting a monarch sipping nectar from your carefully tended butterfly weed—these are the bonuses that only gardeners can enjoy on a regular basis. Be sure to take the time from your chores to get close to the natural world.

unusual plants

right: Look closely at your plants. Trilliums, for instance, with their tripartite configuration—three leaves, three sepals, and three petals—are worth a leisurely study. So are the tiny blooms that make up the flat-topped yarrow inflorescence (flower), the spurred flowers of columbine, and the beautiful falls and standards of an iris.

seasonal changes

below: In spring, fiddleheads emerge and gradually mature to the familiar lacy fronds we know as ferns. Some plants, such as balloon flowers, keep their presence unknown until much later—sometimes endangering their existence because we forget where we planted them the previous year.

statements

right: In addition to demanding attention with their color or fragrance, some plants show off with their particular form. Consider peonies, which have such noticeable yellow stamens, and purple coneflowers with their jaunty, dark, central disk. Such discoveries add to the pleasure of gardening.

planning the details

As you can see, there are probably as many aspects of gardening to notice as there are perennials to plant. Take into consideration the variety of shapes, colors, and fragrances that appeal to you, and think about how they might also entice and nurture wildlife. Think in terms of seasons: the clear greens of newly emerging foliage in spring, the forms of flowers in summer (low-growing, tall, single-flowered, or very double), and the changing hues of flowers and foliage in fall.

You can combine many different interests in one garden. To be successful, all you need to do in the beginning is think small and focus on a few different plants at a time. Don't go wild in your enthusiasm at first because you can—and undoubtedly will—enlarge a border and add plants as you learn more about them.

bird feasts

above: Seed-producing plants, such as purple coneflowers and ornamental grasses, entice birds to visit, and occasionally stay year-round in a garden.

butterfly gems

left: The jewels of the air justify our planting for them simply by being there. Plants such as beebalm, gayfeather, and yarrow will bring butterflies to your yard.

fragrance

above: The ephemeral aspect of perennials is their fragrance. Many entice with their aromas: peonies, iris, lilies, dianthus, phlox, salvias, sweet woodruff. Even those that aren't technically fragrant, like ferns, have a fresh scent that makes you want to reach out and brush them as you pass by.

the gardens

cottage gardens

zones	exposure
4–9	sun or light shade

casual chic

Based on the heritage of English gardening, cottage-style designs might look casual and unplanned, but in reality, they take careful thought and a few years of growth to be truly beautiful. Basically, a cottage garden consists of a combination of perennials, shrubs (such as roses and camellias), and bulbs (for spring

a classic design

right and below: **One of the joys of a cottage-style garden is the abundance of lush, changing colors over a long season. Foxgloves, hollyhocks, daisies, roses, and an arbor set the style in this garden.**

perennials

1 ox-eye daisy, page 117

2 salvia, page 122

3 foxglove, page 113

4 yellow loosestrife, page 118

other plants

a 'joseph's coat' rose

classic arbor

above: **An arbor with seat provides a place for plants to climb and for you to sit to survey the results of your efforts.**

and summer color). Add ornamental grasses and a few perennial herbs, if you wish. You will undoubtedly want to put in some structures: an arbor, perhaps a fence as a backdrop, or a garden bench. While the garden is establishing itself, fill in vacant spaces with annual flowers.

in the beginning

The carefree beauty of your garden requires good site selection, soil preparation, and plants that are appropriate for your climate zone. The size of the garden depends on the size of your property and the amount of time you can devote to it. Carefree does not mean maintenance–free. Taking care of the garden gives you opportunities to enjoy it up close and personal.

cottage gardens

time	skill
weekend	experienced

you will need

- protractor, T square, triangle
- five 2×4s (for rafters)
- saber saw and carpenter's level
- mending plates or corrugated fasteners
- scrap lumber and string (temporary supports)
- posthole digger
- gravel
- four 10'-long 4×4 posts (redwood, red cedar, or pressure-treated lumber)
- ten 1×2s (for crossbars), length as desired
- 1×8 (spacer)
- galvanized nails and screws
- hammer and screwdriver
- wood preservative (optional)

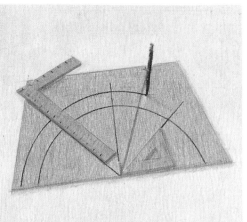

1

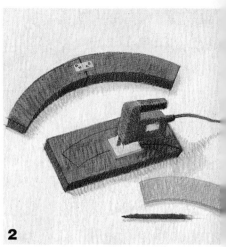

2

3

1   **plan** Use a protractor and T square to draw the curved section of the arbor on paper. The 8-foot tall arbor can be any width you want; 4 feet or wider is best.

2   **cut arch** Trace the pattern onto 2×4s. Cut out four sections for each side of the top using a sabersaw, and temporarily fasten the sections together using mending plates or corrugated fasteners.

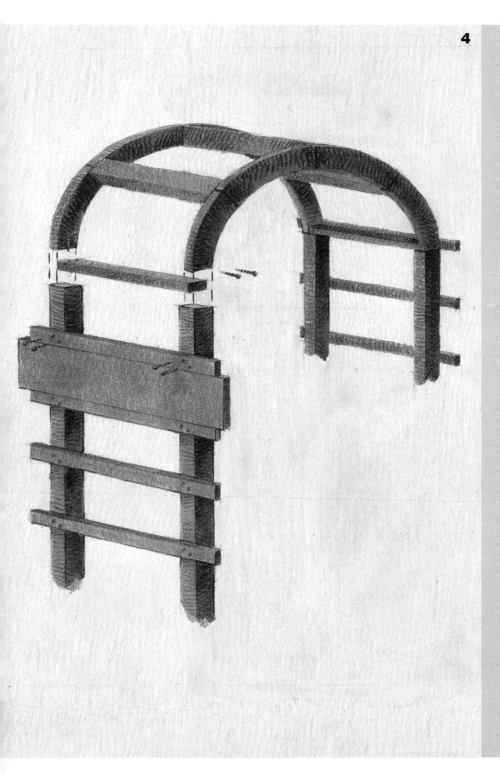

site posts Mark the exact location for **3**
the posts. Drive pegs in at all four corners,
winding string tightly around them. Check
that the sides are parallel and the front and
back square to the sides. Remove the pegs
and dig 2-foot holes with a posthole digger.
Fill bottom of holes with 4 inches of gravel
and insert the posts. Nail temporary supports
between the posts to hold the posts in place
while you pack soil into holes for stability.
Remove the supports and stakes after nailing
on the first crossbars.

arch and spacing Nail one 2×4 to **4**
the top of each side. Screw the two joined
arch pieces to the ends of the 2×4s, making
sure that the mending posts are on the
inside. Then nail a crossbar over each 2×4 to
cover it. Nail the first crossbars 12 inches
above the ground, using a level to ensure
they are even and parallel to each other.
After you attach the first crossbar, place a
1×8 on top of it, rest the next crossbar on it,
and nail the crossbar in place with two nails
for each side. Use the board as a guide to
space the remaining side crossbars evenly.
Screw three rafters between the two arches—
one at each of the three arch "joints." (Notch
the ends of the rafters to accommodate the
mending plates.)

Sand any rough edges. Treat exposed ends
with a wood preservative.

entry gardens

planning your entryway

Front-yard gardens usually show off your best efforts. Here are a few guidelines that will help make the most of your planning and work.

Coordinate the style of your entry garden with that of the house. To ensure that its design adds to the beauty of the house rather than detracts from it, consider both as one entity. Almost any style of garden can enhance a Colonial, English, or French design. A wild or cottage look is inappropriate for a contemporary or a Victorian-style house. Similarly, a very formal garden would look wrong around a Cape Cod or Saltbox house.

Aim for an open view along the walkway from the street to the front door as well as across the

a warm welcome

right and below: **The North American way of planting a front-yard garden is turning away from the mundane foundation plantings of junipers, rhododendrons, and yews, which block windows in a matter of years or take hours of pruning to stay within bounds. Instead, the emphasis is on the unusual—the seasonal interest that colorful perennials provide. Delphiniums and foxgloves provide height and are airy enough to see through.**

perennials

1 delphinium, page 112

2 artemisia, page 107

3 dianthus, page 112

4 marguerite, page 117

5 cranesbill, page 114

other plants

a sweet alyssum

b climbing rose

c petunia

d geranium

front of the house. For a sense of privacy, intersperse tall plants among shorter, bushier ones, especially in front of windows. Tall and airy perennials, such as delphiniums, foxgloves, lilies, and bugbane, interrupt a view; they do not obstruct it.

Build an entry or foundation planting with year-round appearance in mind because it must be a garden for all seasons. Place a few evergreen shrubs strategically to provide structure and interest in seasons when the perennials are dormant. Set tall shrubs near corners; place low-growing ones among the perennials or as a backdrop for them.

Consider exposure and the amount of direct sun your entry receives. With a north or northeast exposure, you might need to augment perennials with annuals, small trees, and groundcovers because many shade-loving perennials bloom only in spring.

country look

right: A fairly narrow bed along the foundation in front of a long, low house adds seasonal color as well as year-round structure and interest. Foxgloves, delphiniums, bellflowers, and lilies mix with annual begonias, candytuft, cosmos, and zinnias. Backed by broad-leaved evergreens, the border is more interesting than the old-fashioned foundation plantings of shrubs you may be used to seeing. Window boxes filled with pansies, nasturtiums, and lobelia provide even more color for the summer months. The abundant plantings—reminiscent of a cutting garden—camouflage the dying foliage of spring-flowering bulbs, which begin the show in April with daffodils and grape hyacinths and continue it into May with tulips. Remember all the seasons of the year when you design a garden, whether the planting is in the front, side, or back. Include evergreen material so the bed has color and interest year round.

contrasting colors

left: Reds, yellows, and white brighten an entry corner. Lilies, black-eyed Susans, and penstemons provide summer color, and evergreen dwarf Alberta spruces and yews provide the planting structure through the winter months.

warm shades

below: Layers of color greet passersby and visitors at the entry garden of this English-style house. The warm hue of the fieldstone and the stark contrast of the white stucco form the backdrop for a kaleidoscope of multicolor roses, foxgloves, and calla lilies, contained in raised beds by a low wall of matching stone. The lush bed on the right, backed by a higher stone wall, hides a small patio from the view of the street.

beautiful borders

zones	exposure
4–9	sun or light shade

color

Consider how colors affect the overall feel of the garden. Blues and violets are receding, cool colors, making a garden seem larger. Bold reds, oranges, and yellows are warm colors; too much can overwhelm a small plot.

Group colors and plants and repeat them along the length of the border. Because of the differences in flower and leaf shapes and growth habits, the grouping of white iris, peonies, and columbines, *right,* for example, has a larger impact than an equal-size planting of only one of these species,

border basics

right: **For beauty as well as ease of maintenance, plant your borders with perennials; use annuals to fill in empty spaces and provide edging with continuous bloom. To achieve a balanced design, plan the garden on paper first.**

shape

Use a mix of plant shapes: mat (dianthus), cushion (euphorbia), mounded (sedum), narrow (fountain grass), strap-shape (iris), airy (baby's breath), and spiky (veronica).

Vary the shape and texture of foliage because few perennials bloom for an entire season. Choose foliage that is an attribute when the flowers are gone. Leaves may be coarse (bergenia) or fine (meadow rue), rounded (hosta) or lance-shape (coreopsis), glossy (black snakeroot) or velvety (lamb's-ears), variegated (heliopsis) or silver (artemisia).

perennials

1 peony, page 119

2 columbine, page 107

3 bearded iris, page 130

4 foxglove, page 113

other plants

a impatiens

beautiful borders

border know-how

For the most impressive planting, make your garden as deep as 6 feet. That may seem large, but it will provide enough space for bigger, varied plantings. A 6- to 9-foot depth is room to layer groups of plants—from lowest to tallest—rather than to string out several individual specimens.

The garden may look sparse when you first plant it, but within two to three years, the perennials will spread to cover the vacant spaces. Resist the impulse to set plants closer than the recommended mature spacing. Most perennials will grow 2 to 3 feet or more in circumference. If you crowd plants when they are young, they are less likely to be healthy (without the benefit of good air circulation around them), and you will need to dig them up and divide them before too long.

To access all of the areas of a deep border,

1 early summer For bounteous color all season, select perennials that bloom early, midseason, and late. At the beginning of summer, you might select black-eyed Susans, coreopsis, daylilies, blanket flowers, and lilies. Edge the border with low-growing annuals that will flower all season: marigolds, ageratum, petunias, and zinnias. You may want to choose a color scheme for each season and use that color as a backbone of the garden.

2 midsummer For midsummer, when temperatures are hottest and water may be scarce, add cooling colors. Clumps of white and pink phlox with blue and purple delphinium and veronica contribute eye-pleasing shades as well as vertical accents to the garden. Other good bloomers include balloon flower, scabiosa, lavender, cupid's dart, butterfly weed, globe thistle, bugbane, and beebalm.

3 fall Chrysanthemums are most important for continued color in the garden from late summer through fall. Blue-flowered asters and hardy ageratum, yellow-flowered goldenrod and helianthus, purple-flushed turtlehead, and rosy obedient plant contribute autumn blooms as well. Fall is the season when you may be most aware of foliage shape, texture, and color, from hostas and coralbells to artemisia and ornamental grasses.

place stepping-stones or pavers strategically for an integral, pleasing part of the design.

beyond plants

There is more to a good border design than plants. In addition to a few stepping stones, you might want to lay an informal path to bisect the border so you can walk right into the garden. Create another destination by setting an arbor or a bench at the end of the path.

Augment perennials with decorative containers of annuals and small shrubs. Invite birds into the border with a birdbath secluded among medium or tall plants.

Selectively—*very selectively*—place statues or other works of art into the garden. Edge the border, if you want, with a low barrier of wrought iron, terra-cotta, or wood. Or spade a trench to keep the perimeter neat and the border clear of the roots of invading grass and weeds.

shade gardens

zones	exposure
4–9	shade or light shade

planning

The kind of garden you can plant depends on the type of shade you have, the growth habit of the surrounding trees and shrubs, and the soil characteristics. Perennials must

subtle beauty

right and below: **Perennials for shade gardens are exquisite. Many bloom in spring before the trees leaf out and create a covering canopy. Quite a few, such as the astilbe and leopard plant (not yet blooming), flower in summer. Like the hosta and fern, their foliage is so attractive that the plants deserve a place in the garden even if they never flowered.**

perennials

1 astilbe, page 108

2 leopard plant, page 117

3 fern, pages 126–127

4 hosta, page 116

other plants

a wintercreeper

compete with the trees for moisture, nutrients, and space, so it is easier to plant under deep-rooted trees, such as oaks, than under shallow-rooted maples. Damp shade supports more plants than dry shade. High canopies allow more sun to reach the plants than low-branching evergreens. Raise the canopy by pruning off the lowest limbs. Deciduous trees allow sun into the garden in early to midspring, which is an advantage for selecting plants, but observe how the light quality and intensity change before you plant.

selecting plants

Foliage texture and color are most important in a shade garden. Flowers are ephemeral; foliage brings substance and interest to the area for the longest season.

shade gardens

plants for shady gardens

Think of the various shades of green: chartreuse, bluish, grayish, pale, dark. Envision leaves edged with cream, white, yellow, or burgundy. Contemplate those with smooth, crinkled, and puckered textures; plants with simple or very bisected; rounded, heart-shape, or spiky; small or gigantic leaves.

Add flowers, however brief their season, and such a garden will bring lovely, cool, and soothing aspects to the yard.

plants that like shade

- astilbe
- hardy begonia
- bleeding heart
- columbine
- coralbells
- corydalis
- dead nettle
- ferns
- hellebore
- hosta
- jacob's ladder
- lungwort
- primrose
- sweet woodruff
- virginia bluebells
- wild ginger

shady colors

opposite: Sweet woodruff carpets the ground along a woodland walk beside a stream. The shade garden is filled with rhododendrons, azaleas, ferns, and iris.

far left: Cinnamon fern and white-flowered wood anemones grow in the shade of a silverbell tree.

left: Delicate yellow blooms of corydalis, a plant for sun or light shade, brighten a corner filled with hostas.

below: In moist soil in light shade, yellow flag blooms with ferns and hostas—all three do well in damp locations.

naturalistic gardens

zones	exposure
3–10	sun

worth a garden

Birds love natural gardens because they can find all they need to survive in them. Seed heads of perennials and ornamental grasses provide food. Shrubs, trees, and some perennials offer shelter and nesting places. A birdbath contains water for drinking and bathing. You, meanwhile, gain the benefit of natural pest control because many birds eat hundreds of insects daily.

When you plan a natural wildlife garden, include a diverse selection of plants—trees, shrubs, grasses, perennials, and annuals that reseed. Birds and other wildlife won't care if you have the latest cultivars; in fact, they prefer species and older varieties. Look for plants indigenous to your area, because they will look the most natural in it.

back to nature

right and below: **The wild, somewhat unkempt look of a naturalistic garden is misleading. The garden takes as much planning as a formal design does. It also requires preliminary work—weed removal, good soil preparation, and appropriate plant selection. The rewards are in the seasonal changes you can observe in the plants, such as these grasses and sedum, and the wildlife visitors you will see flying and creeping around.**

perennials

1 'autumn joy' sedum, page 123

2 russian sage, page 120

3 feather reed grass, page 128

4 pampas grass, page 128

maintenance

Be less than vigilant about grooming the garden and the plants. Let many of the flowers go to seed, especially late in the season, to provide birds a source of food. Pull out or transplant seedlings that germinate too prolifically or in places you don't want them. Wait until the following spring to cut back the plumes of ornamental grasses rather than cutting them in autumn.

Be careful about using any kind of pesticide in the garden. When you must use one, do so at night when birds will not be foraging for food.

You may not love all the wildlife your garden attracts. Raccoons and groundhogs can be a nuisance and might eat your vegetables and flowers. Deer are difficult to protect against. Be prepared to share some of your favorite flowers and vegetables with nature's creatures.

glorious grasses
above: Ornamental grasses—ruby-colored fountain grass, Japanese blood grass, and sedge—and salvias are easy-care plants that provide cover and food for birds and other small animals.

cooling effects
right: Hot, dry sites can be floriferous if you take advantage of the shade cast by deciduous trees and shrubs.

long-lived plants

left: Purple coneflower and coreopsis form a delightful complementary pair in any garden. The color contrast is particularly effective in the wildflower look of a naturalistic design.

bird friendly

below left: A lush garden with salvias (*Salvia coccinea* and *S. leucantha*), 'Powis Castle' artemisia, and tall, purple-spired fountain grass surrounds a dovecote. Species of salvia are especially attractive to hummingbirds, as are the jasmine flowers covering the tuteur on the left. You may see wrens, chickadees, and titmice balancing on the waving stems of the grass.

sunny color

below: For a sunny border, black-eyed Susans, sedum, purple coneflower, and blue-flowered Russian sage make neat clumps of color. These plants are not invasive. All of them have a long bloom season, and their flowers or seed heads last well into winter, providing a natural source of food for birds that do not fly away to warmer climates.

time	skill
1–2 hours	easy

you will need

hoe or shovel

protective gear: rubber gloves, safety glasses, dust mask

spray bottle and water

3 gallons premixed concrete

peat moss

crushed, colored, recycled glass

rock specimens

sheet of plastic

for songbirds

This special handmade birdbath belongs nestled in a flower bed where admirers will never know that it was so easy to make. You don't need a fancy mold to fashion the 18- to 20-inch basin. You can even use a cardboard box instead of the ground, as long as the box is at least 4 inches wider than the basin's width. Fill it 10 inches deep with soil; then scoop a basin shape in the soil.

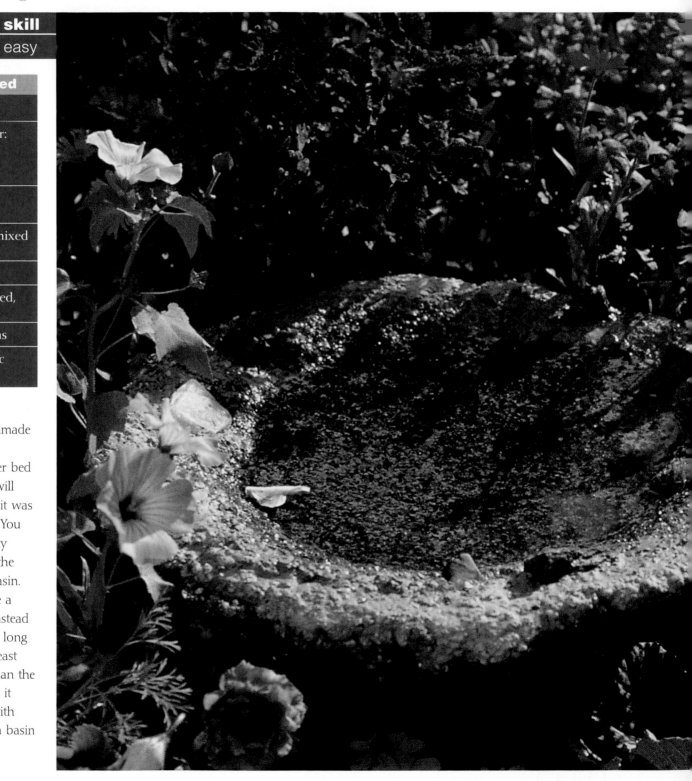

1 mold Dig and shape a hole in the ground (or in a cardboard box filled with 10 inches of soil) as a mold. Sprinkle the shape with water and pack down the soil firmly. Tamp a flat area in the center so the finished basin will sit securely on a flat surface.

2 mix Wear protective gear. Combine 3 gallons of premixed concrete with 2 to 3 cups of peat moss in a wheelbarrow. Add about 2 gallons of water and quickly mix with a hoe to make a stiff batter. If it is too thin, add more concrete; if too thick to hold together, add water.

3 form Work quickly, concrete starts to set in minutes. Shovel the wet mix into the mold. Scoop concrete from the center of the basin to the outside rim. Pat it into place, conforming it to the shape of the basin. Pat smooth. Spritz with water to keep concrete moist.

4 finish Decorate the basin by sprinkling crushed, recycled glass on the wet mix; press gently into place. You also can use other decorative pieces such as stones. Cover the basin with a plastic sheet; let cure for 3 to 7 days. Uncover; let age for 1 month before filling with water.

butterfly gardens

zones	exposure
4–10	sun

warmth and water

Butterflies need the warmth of the sun and appreciate a flat stone or two for basking. You will see them gather in groups if you provide a shallow puddle where they can drink. Protect them from strong

winged jewels

right and below:
Butterflies are a delight to watch as they float around the garden on a breeze, alighting briefly on nodding flowers. Attract them by planting a few perennials and shrubs for their larval needs and more for their nectar preferences, such as the beard-tongue, catmint, crambe, and veronica in this garden.

perennials

1 iris, pages 130–131

2 catmint, page 119

3 oriental poppy, page 120

4 speedwell, page 125

5 beard-tongue, page 120

6 foxglove, page 113

7 bellflower, page 110

8 crambe, page 111

winds with a garden near a few shrubs or trees that act as a windbreak.

plan the beauty

You can incorporate butterfly plants into an existing bed or border, such as that at left, or plant a separate garden. To a butterfly, fragrance is not as important as color, although it does play a role. The eyes of a butterfly perceive a shades of yellow, red, and blue to lavender.

The best flowering plants for a butterfly garden are wild or species forms rather than hybrids, single-flowered instead of double-flowered, and tubular or flat-topped.

Plant in large groups; individual spots of color are less attractive than a broad wash of hues. Groups of 10 or more of the same color work well.

butterfly gardens

two winners

right: Beebalm and purple coneflower are two of the best plants for attracting butterflies. Plant groups of them around a weathered fountain, and shelter the garden with a backdrop of evergreens.

nectar and food plants

below: In July, large groups of colorful purple coneflower, phlox, gayfeather, beebalm, Shasta daisy, and black-eyed Susan mingle in a wild garden. Less colorful but almost as important are larval plants. Some butterflies are quite plant-specific, laying eggs on one type of plant. Monarchs, for example, lay their eggs only on milkweed. Others are more opportunistic, using a range of plants, from herbs such as dill and parsley, to trees such as cherry and tulip poplar. Include trees elsewhere in the yard if you do not want to incorporate them in the garden bed.

plants that attract butterflies

- anise hyssop
- beebalm
- black-eyed susan
- butterfly weed
- coreopsis
- dianthus
- garden phlox
- purple coneflower
- queen anne's lace
- red valerian
- thyme
- vervain

juicy fruit
above: Butterflies like sweet fruit. Put a slice of ripe papaya, orange, or banana near the edge of the garden and you can watch them feed.

nectar blooms
far left: Butterfly weed is a favorite nectar plant. Although there are new cultivars in various colors, stick to the species to attract butterflies to the garden.

rest stop
left: The jury is still out on the usefulness of butterfly houses. If the house doesn't lure them, the arching butterfly bush will.

multiseason interest

zones	exposure
3–9	sun or light shade

season to season
The beauty of a garden is not confined to one, two, or even three seasons. Whether you are out in its midst or gazing at it through a window, you want to see something attractive in the garden all year. With a bit of planning, you can.

looking ahead
right and below: The beauty of a winter garden depends on the details: foliage and stem color, ever-present structure—from seed heads on perennials, and evergreen branches on conifers to accessories, such as benches—and play of light and shadow as the sun moves lower in the sky.

perennials
1 sedge, page 128

2 zebra grass, page 129

3 sedum, page 123

other plants
a spruce

b red twig dogwood

c fir

Color during the growing season, spring to fall, relies not only on flowers but also on foliage. Think of the dusky maroon leaves of some coralbells and 'Vera Jameson' sedum, the variegations of hostas and euonymus, the silver-gray of artemisia and lamb's ears, the red of Japanese blood grass, and the blue of blue oat grass. For winter, plant red- or yellow-stemmed dogwoods and berried shrubs or trees (roses, hollies, crabapples). The bright reds will seem to shimmer when backlit by the setting sun.

Pattern refers to leaf shapes as well as branch and growth habits. Although the leaves may be most noticeable in summer, the plant's habit takes on importance in winter when a dusting of snow accentuates it. Perennials left in the garden for winter, such as grasses, sedums, coneflowers, look wonderful topped with snow. Leafless branches of deciduous trees show the intricate designs you miss during the summer months; their shadows on lawns and snow are an integral part of the special quality a garden takes on in winter.

Structure includes the permanent parts of your garden: fences, arbors, trellises, rock outcroppings, and evergreen plantings. In many zones, perennials such as sea thrift, bergenia, and coralbells are evergreen, but for assured year-round interest, add shrubs such as boxwood, and ornamental grasses, such as fountain grass and maiden grass, to give the garden form.

multiseason interest

winter

right: A good reason to be a little lazy when it comes to cleaning up the garden in fall is the presence that leftover plants lend to the landscape. Witness the fountain grass and sedum here, with snow capping their dried and drooping flower heads, and the coneflowers with their dark seed heads. Permanent elements, such as the brick path, provide a link to the garden design.

early summer

below: Start calling attention to this garden in early summer. These late-blooming plants don't get much notice in spring. That is the time to cut down the old sedum bloom stalks and the ornamental grasses. You could interplant spring-flowering bulbs, which would add early-season color among the perennials.

summer

left: At the height of the gardening season, color and shape abound. Delightful purple coneflower and bright black-eyed Susan contrast with the warm, celery-green flowers of 'Autumn Joy' sedum and the blue spires of Russian sage. Ornamental grasses (such as fountain grass) and daylilies provide vertical accents with their strap-shape leaves. The texture of the plumes on grasses adds to the garden design.

autumn

left: The fall season brings subtle color to the garden, interspersed with warm shades of oranges, yellows, and reds from sedums and chrysanthemums. This is the season for purple-blue asters and the tans and beiges of the fluffy plumes of ornamental grasses. Even as you cut back other perennials that have stopped blooming, enjoy the interplay of garden colors with those of the changing fall leaves on deciduous trees. Evergreen—or ever-colored—plants, such as purple-leaved coralbells, reveal their benefits in a multiseason garden.

hillside gardens

zones	exposure
3–10	sun

thwart erosion

Aside from the difficulty of trying to mow a hill or slope, you have the problems of drainage (too much, too fast) and soil erosion. Many plants, including perennials, help stabilize the soil. Grasses are among them, but turfgrass requires much work to maintain. Ornamental grasses, on the other hand, are often drought-tolerant, and need to be cut back once a year in spring. No lawn mower needed.

Good grasses for hillsides include many you would not want to put into a border because they can

rolling on

right: A hillside—whether rocky, screelike, steep, or gentle—might not be an ideal place for a lawn. Turn it into a lovely garden like this with a variety of flowering groundcovers with texture and foliage that provide interest after the flowers have faded.

become invasive. On a slope, their rampant growth and spread is fine. Sweet flag, switch grass, buffalograss, and ribbon grass are a few. Add some clumping grasses, such as fountain grass, oat grass, and little bluestem, and a few heaths, heathers, and creeping junipers for an attractive solution to a potential problem.

special gardens

Large rocks embedded in a gentle slope form microclimates that can create the perfect spot for special plants (such as alpines, cacti, and succulents) that might not survive in your climate under regular garden conditions.

plants

1 dianthus, page 112

2 sedum, page 123

3 speedwell, page 125

4 cranesbill, page 114

5 stone cress, page 106

6 snow-in-summer, page 110

7 aubretia, page 108

gentle slope

above left: An informal layering of bluestone holds in the soil at the bottom of this gentle slope and provides the perfect ledge for candytuft to spill over. Colorful yellow coreopsis, blue catmint, and silvery artemisia offer a long season of contrasts.

narrow access

above right: You can dress up even the narrowest bed, such as this one between two sets of stairs leading to a pair of Berkeley, California townhouses, with a variety of hardy succulents, including flowering jade, aloe, and crassulas.

steep ascent

right: Retaining walls made with the same stone as the stairs offer pockets for planting on this steep hillside. Low-growing, ground-covering shrubs guarantee that the beds will look good in all seasons, not only in summer. Bright spots of color— from annuals such as begonias and petunias to perennial groundcovers—turn the hillside into a lush, vibrant landscape.

stair softening

left: Very steep hillsides usually require a series of steps to make access easier. You can soften the stark look of stone, wood, or cement stairs if you leave a trough at the back of each tread and place creeping plants, such as thyme, baby's tears, and sedums, into it to spread over part of the steps. Set hostas, low-growing grasses, sedges, or ferns along the stairway to drape over the steps. Do not let the plants cover so much of the surface, however, that they threaten users' safety.

sedum subtleties

below: Sedums and sempervivums are excellent plants for rocky hillsides. Their various shades of green harmonize with early-blooming perennials, such as pink-flowered stone cress and cranesbill. Sedums are not invasive, and they are tolerant of drought and less-than-ideal soils and growing conditions—all three situations that they are likely to contend with on hilly locations.

perennial gardens | **47**

xeriscape gardens

zones	exposure
5–11	sun or light shade

characteristics

Xeriscaping, using plants that have little or no need for water other than what rains provide, is adaptable to any section of the country. Focus on native wildflowers, trees,

look—no water

right and below:
Gardening without water or with water restrictions does not mean gardening without the beauty of flowers and the tantalizing effects of texture and form. You don't have to limit yourself to cacti and succulents (hardy or not), as beautiful as they are in this textural garden.

perennials

1 myrtle spurge, page 114
2 aeonium, page 106
3 prickly pear, page 119
4 hedgehog cactus, page 120

other plants

a buckwheat
b calylophis

and shrubs that have acclimated themselves to local growing conditions over the centuries. You might find that the allure of cacti is irresistible, especially after you have seen their bright, shimmering spring blooms next to crocus, grape hyacinth, and iris.

under the surface

Soil preparation, which is important for any garden, is paramount for a Xeriscape. The seemingly contradictory ability of the soil to retain water and also drain well is one of the secrets of dryscape gardening success. Plants that can withstand drought (cacti and succulents), many wildflowers (such as black-eyed Susan), and most ornamental grasses do not survive in standing water. Build up layers of gravel and grit before spreading a mix of sand, gravel, and soil on top, especially if you want to grow hardy cacti. Form the soil into mounds 4 to 5 inches high for the plants to grow on. Mulch with a ½-inch layer of stones and gravel.

garden oases

right: Take advantage of the microclimates you can create within a larger landscape. Here, dwarf conifers, alpines, and green and variegated iris survive heat and drought in summer; chives, prickly pears, and ornamental grasses take on winter cold—in a bed filled with amended soil to improve drainage and topped with stones to reflect light and absorb warmth. Group plants with similar needs (for example, a lot of direct sun or not much moisture) to make your maintenance chores easier.

hardy cacti

above: Opuntia, also known as rabbit ear, cholla, and prickly pear, is one of many cacti that will grow in cool climates. This pink form of *Opuntia basilaris* var. *aurea* is in a Detroit garden. Other cacti worth trying are the rather small columnar *Echinocereus* spp., with their large blooms, the pincushion cacti, *Coryphantha* spp., and other opuntia, from miniatures and shrublike bushes to *Opuntia compressa*—one of the hardiest.

warm-season color

left: Use touches of contrast to brighten a basically one-color garden. Here, a cutleaf Japanese maple anchors the corner of a bed filled with iris, feather grass, and lilyturf. Plant forms offer another opportunity for contrast—the grasslike foliage of lilyturf and the strap-shape leaves of the iris.

contemplative gardens

zones	exposure
3–11	light shade

the elements

To design a garden that is a cool and inviting retreat, consider including a gravel path; water in the form of a simple fountain, pond, stream, or birdbath; stone statuary; moss for soft texture and attractive color; evergreen and spring-flowering trees and shrubs; and perennials that will provide foliage interest after flowering.

Use plants that will give the effect of bamboo. Heavenly bamboo (*Nandina domestica),* which isn't a bamboo but a relative of barberry, has the bonus of red berries in fall and winter.

peaceful spots

right: Contemplative gardens contain subtle colors. With a long heritage of Oriental horticultural practices, these gardens might be variations on shades of green, with few if any flowers. A small water feature, such as this bamboo fountain, is often included.

Ornamental grasses, such as fountain and maiden grass, and reeds catch a breeze like bamboo does.

about bamboo

If you use bamboo, select clump-forming species instead of running bamboos, which require a fortresslike barrier (a 2- to 3-foot deep concrete edging) to prevent their taking over the yard. Clump-forming bamboos spread, but not as quickly or invasively. Among the most winter hardy are purple-tinted fountain bamboo (*Sinarundinaria nitida*, hardy to Zone 5) and yellow-green umbrella bamboo (*Thamnocalamus spathaceus*, hardy to Zone 6).

perennials

1 lilyturf, page 118
2 bamboo, page 129
3 bowles golden sedge, page 128

other plants

a japanese maple

contemplative gardens

shady retreats

right: Because it is difficult to be at ease for very long in the glaring sun, site your contemplative retreat in the shade. You can create a shady spot with plantings of bamboo or evergreen trees and shrubs or by enclosing the spot with a tall fence. (Bamboo makes a natural fence in one year of growth.) Add one or two spring-flowering trees, such as dogwood or redbud, and a deciduous tree, such as Japanese cutleaf or red maple, for brilliant fall color.

Foliage shapes, textures, and colors and plant forms are important. Bleeding heart, angel's trumpet, ferns, gunnera, hostas, iris, jack-in-the-pulpit, Japanese anemone, trillium, Solomon's seal, and Hakone grass will bring a variety of growth habits and flower colors to your garden from spring to late summer.

Make paths with wood rounds, small-size gravel or grit, or fine mulch so the paths will blend naturally with the surrounding garden.

quiet seating

above left: A bench sheltered among trees and leafy perennials is de rigueur. It provides a destination as well as a place to sit and think.

pleasant access

above right: A simple or a zigzag bridge—over a dry creek or a flowing stream—directs your passage and offers varying garden views.

artful visions

left: You'll usually find water in these gardens, whether in the form of a pond, a fountain, or a gentle waterfall. The sound of water masks street noises; the surface of still water creates a canvas onto which plant reflections are painted.

evening gardens

zones	exposure
3–9	sun or light shade

garden for your time

You undoubtedly know about the four-o-clock, which opens its pink, red, or yellow buds in late afternoon, and the annual moonflower (relative of the day-blooming morning glory). There are, however, many

enjoy the garden

right and below: It's all very well to design beautiful gardens, but if they are lovely to look at only during daylight hours, they won't satisfy you if you're not home to see them. That's where evening gardens come to the rescue. They contain plants that blossom in the evening or have light-colored flowers that shine through in the darkness.

perennials

1 white bleeding heart, page 112

2 hellebore (lenten rose), page 115

3 christmas rose, page 115

4 trillium, page 125

5 european ginger, page 108

perennials whose scent is stronger or color more vibrant than in daylight hours that belong in an evening garden. Some flowers are showier in the subdued light of dusk.

coloring it up

Plants with silver or gray foliage (lamb's ears, dusty miller, artemisia, some coralbells varieties) belong in the garden. White flowers (lily, Shasta daisy, garden phlox, gooseneck loosestrife, yarrow, flowering tobacco, and feverfew) provide the classic color of an evening garden. Accents of pink (evening primrose and foxglove), blue (gayfeather and salvia), and yellow (daylily and 'Moonbeam' coreopsis) stand out in relief against the subtle monochromatic palette of silver and white. White-flowered annuals, such as sweet alyssum, geranium, petunia, snapdragon, and zinnia, contribute brightness to an evening garden.

seasonal scenes from a garden—early spring

right: A garden next to a porch offers comfortable opportunities for enjoying an evening garden. Select flowers that remain open at dusk: delphiniums in shades of white and pale blue; columbines in white, blue and white, and rose; astilbes with deep rose, pink, red, and white spires of blooms; and daylilies (there are varieties that stay open in the evening, in spite of their name).

midspring color

below: White is the color of choice for many evening gardens because its various shades bring the area to life—and sight—as the sun sets. White is also one of the most common colors in nature, whether it is in western bleeding heart, foamflower, candytuft, or roses such as 'Iceberg', 'Alba' and 'Ice' Meidiland, and 'Madame Hardy'. Scatter other colors among the whites; they will pop out against the neutral background. And always remember foliage—the different shapes and textures add dimension to the garden.

late-spring fragrance
above: Peonies are wonderful in any garden because of their large, gorgeous, fragrant blooms and their foliage, which sets off other plants throughout the season. Pale rose foxgloves will seem to glow in the evening next to creamy white columbines. Include other flowers with fragrance, such as dianthus, clematis, annual stock, four-o-clock, and vining moonflower, with its huge blooms. Scents tend to be much stronger in the evening.

raised beds

alternatives

Instead of coping with the inevitable erosion on uneven ground, such as that on a slope or rocky hillside, you can terrace the land with stone walls to create aesthetically pleasing raised beds that make attractive gardens near sunken patios and along paths.

preplanning

If you build a raised bed or wall yourself, lay stones without mortar (dry stone construction) and

above ground

right: Of the many reasons for creating a garden above the ground, one of the most critical is waterlogged soil; few plants survive well in constantly boggy soil. Another is the soil itself. In this clay hillside, it was more practical to build a raised bed and bring in good loam than to amend the poor soil.

limit the height of the wall to 3 feet. It can, of course, be shorter, as low as 12 inches high.

Use mostly flat stones; they make the construction rather like laying bricks. The weight of each course or layer of stones will help hold the stones in place. Tilting back the stones slightly also will help because the soil filled in the bed will secure them.

If you plan to plant in the crevices, fill the spaces with soil as you build. Set the plants in the soil when you have finished the wall.

plants

1 blue oat grass, page 129

2 thyme, page 124

3 sedum, page 123

raised beds: building a stone wall

zones	time	skill
4–8	2–4 days	moderate

you will need

- garden hose or rope
- spray paint
- shovel
- stakes
- carpenter's level
- string
- flat rocks, various sizes

filling it up

When you finished the wall, fill the bed with fertile soil enriched with organic matter, such as compost. Water well and let the soil settle for a few days to a week before planting.

outdoor dressing

right: Although you can surround a raised bed with a number of different materials, from timber to bricks, a stone wall sets it off naturally. Building a dry stone wall is easier than constructing one with bricks and mortar, and your efforts will last longer than if you used wood.

1 shape Outline the edge of the bed using a rope or a garden hose. When you are pleased with the shape of the design, spray-paint the outline on the ground, so you will have a reference of the space you need to clear for the planting bed.

2 level Set the level of the stone wall by hammering stakes into the ground along the painted line, marking the height of the wall on each stake. Connect the marks with a taut string. Check again to make sure that the top of the wall is level all along its length.

3 stack Remove the grass inside the stakes. Tilt the stones down slightly and back into the bed for stability. To build the wall without mortar, fill the crevices between and behind the stones with soil. Use the string as a guide for height.

4 finish On a sloping site, adjust the string height to compensate for the slope so the finished wall appears level. Finish the top of the wall with large flat stones. If you want plants to grow in the wall, leave crannies for planting as you build.

perennial gardens | **63**

edible treasures

zones	exposure
4–11	sun

perennial edibles

Asparagus and rhubarb are valuable additions to any garden because of their foliage. Asparagus has feathery leaves on stalks that grow 3 to 5 feet tall; use it in the background of a border, as long as you can access the plants to

mix and match

right and below: **There aren't many perennial vegetables—asparagus and rhubarb are two of the best known—but you can fill out a garden with a mix of other perennial edible herbs and flowers, as in this garden.**

perennials

1 thyme, page 124

2 dianthus, page 112

3 chamomile, page 110

4 lemon thyme, page 124

5 allium (chives), page 106

other plants

a nasturtium

b 'lemon gem' marigold

c calendula

harvest the spears. The large leaves of rhubarb make an architectural statement in any garden; use it as a specimen plant or as a focal point in a bed.

tasty selections

Perennial herbs include the tiny-leaved thymes (common, silver, and lemon) and the grayish-green and multicolored sages. Lemon balm, mints (peppermint, spearmint, orange mint, plain, and variegated), oregano, marjoram, rosemary, and lavender bring fragrance and texture to gardens. Plant them in a separate bed or mix them with your other perennial plants.

edible flowers

When you grow flowers to eat or to use as a garnish, never treat them with chemical sprays. Edible flowers include daylilies, scarlet runner beans, pansies, dianthus, calendulas, violets, and tulips, as well as herb flowers and, of course, roses.

scentsational

above: A mass of lavender comes into bloom as the flowers of chives begin to go past their prime. Think of season of bloom when you plan a fragrant or edible garden to have color in succession, just as you do in a border of perennial flowers. For year-round appeal, place an accent piece, such as a birdbath or sundial, centered or slightly off-center in the bed.

kitty comfort

right: Catnip will keep feline friends in ecstasy. A bonus for the gardener is the lovely gray-green shade of the foliage, which can be particularly effective with a background planting of common mint, with its deeper green leaves. Catnip, or catmint, is not as invasive as true mint—one reason being that cats keep it in check; protect it from foragers with a chicken wire enclosure until it becomes well established.

fragrant paths

left: A combination of raised and mulched beds with brick and gravel paths leads visitors to the front door. Texture and form are the emphasis here, although fleeting colors from late-spring and early-summer flowers add temporary interest. Clumps of lavender and oregano contrast with grasslike chives and Egyptian onions as well as with shrublike sage. Add silver and gray accents with the deeply divided leaves of globe artichoke, cardoon, or artemisia or the velvety foliage of lamb's ears.

In a raised-bed garden such as this, you could safely plant mint without fear of it taking over. In the ground, however, you should curtail its invasive tendency to spread by underground runners by planting it in a bottomless pot with the rim just above the soil level.

If you provide sage with ideal growing conditions, it, too, can threaten to take over a garden, but it is easy to restrain by pulling up young plants in spring.

garden paths: brick

zones	time	skill	exposure
3–11	weekend	moderate	sun to light shade

you will need

- shovel
- hose or rope
- porous weed mat (optional)
- pea gravel and builder's sand
- edging (optional)
- bricks
- tamper
- broom

a statement of style

A path can be made from a broad range of materials, but to some extent, your choice will depend on the impression you want to make. In informal and woodland gardens, for example, you may want gravel or mulchlike shredded

perennials

1 corydalis, page 111
2 foxglove, page 113
3 feverfew, page 124
4 ox-eye daisy, page 117
5 iris, page 130

other plants

a 'pjm' rhododendron

bark chips. Formal beds look best with grass paths or those of stone or brick set in mortar.

Setting the material (bricks, stepping–stones, or pavers) in sand instead of concrete or mortar results in an informal look. Such paths are easier and less expensive to lay, and they leave crevices for creeping plants.

A path does not have to be continuous. You can make an attractive path that stops at a focal point and begins again across a lawn or garden bed.

walking about

left: A brick path such as this—or any path in the yard— should not be a last-minute addition. It is more important than a means of getting from one place to another. A well-designed path adds to the overall impact of a garden, so plan carefully for it.

garden paths: brick

1 **design** With the exception of grass, brick paths are the most classic walkways in a garden. You can lay bricks in an amazing array of patterns and shapes, and the laying is relatively easy.

Use a garden hose or rope to lay out the path, making it at least 2 to 3 feet wide. To keep the width accurate, you may want to mark it with paint as you go. If you follow the slope of a slight incline, use a curve or series of loose curves to help reduce the grade; broaden the path sightly where it curves.

2 **dig** Remove the sod and dig the base of the walk for its entire length. The depth should equal the thickness of the brick plus 4 inches for a sand base and 2 inches for gravel. Check the depth as you dig to maintain an even base.

3 **underlay** When you have cleared the path, lay down porous weed mat, if you want, to help keep the path weed-free and to allow rain water to seep through. Shovel in about 2 inches of pea gravel and spread it evenly. Add 4 inches of builder's sand as a base for the bricks. To maintain the original edges of the path, hammer in garden or landscape edging, bending it where necessary to follow the curves of the design.

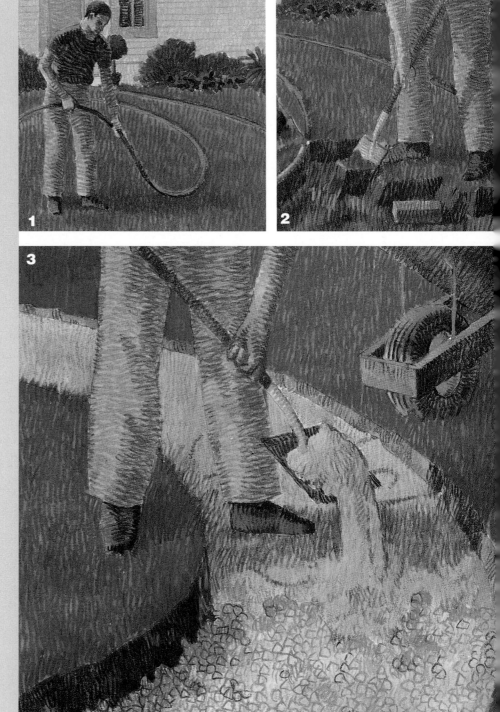

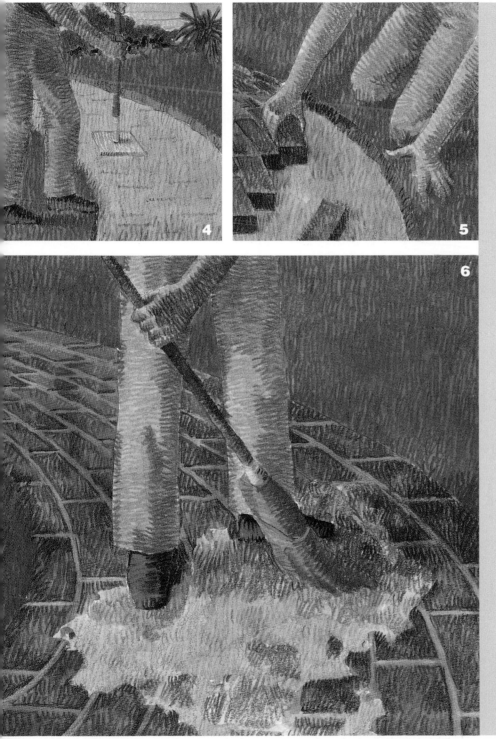

tamp Bricks need a firm, even surface so if you place them, they will lay securely. Tamp the entire sand surface of the path. Use a level to check for accuracy.

4

lay bricks A number of patterns are suitable for brick paths. Running bond, shown here, alternates the ends of the bricks. Stack bond lays each row of bricks evenly and end to end. Herringbone, basket weave, diagonal herringbone, and double basket weave are other attractive patterns. They require more time and skill to lay.

5

If you use old bricks, chip off excess mortar before placing them. Lay the bricks close together, moving in sections along the walk.

settle Pour sand over the bricks and brush it into the crevices between. Brush away the excess. Let the path settle for a few days. You can hose the path with water to help settle the sand in the spaces. Add more sand if necessary. In areas with below-freezing winter weather, the alternate freezing and thawing of the ground beneath might heave some bricks out of place. You might need to reset some of the bricks each year.

6

During the growing season, pull weed seedlings that appear in the path.

garden paths: gravel

zones	time	level	exposure
3–11	weekend	easy	sun to light shade

you will need

- shovel
- porous weed mat
- large stones or pavers
- gravel
- steel-tine rake
- gravel

undercover doings

When you dig out the walk, remove any tree and weed roots and rocks. You might want to lay a 1-inch-deep foundation of sand before you put down a weed mat, but it is not required.

For dry footing, lay a porous weed mat on top of the excavated walk. Do not use a nonporous black-plastic liner because it doesn't allow water to drain away.

Occasionally during the year, perhaps once every season, rake the gravel to smooth it. Blow fallen leaves or debris off the walk in autumn with the low setting on a yard/leaf blower.

simple gravel

right: The most natural-looking path is one created with gravel, pebbles, stones, pine needles, or shredded bark. Gravel and small pebbles are the easiest to walk on. Pine needles can be slippery, especially when they are wet. Shredded bark and stones are often uncomfortable underfoot.

perennials

1 thyme, page 124
2 saxifrage, page 123
3 allium, page 106
4 bellflower, page 110
5 sea pink, white, page 107
6 cranesbill, page 114

1 prepare Dig out the walk: 6 to 8 inches deep and 16 to 36 inches wide. A wider width will allow two people to walk abreast. If you want plants to spill over onto the gravel, make the walk wide enough to accommodate them without impeding foot traffic.

2 edge Place large stones or pavers along both sides of the walk to act as a retaining wall that will separate the gravel from the soil in the planting beds. For the most natural look, use stones that are indigenous to your area.

3 underlay Lay out the weed mat in the walk and cut it to the full width of the path plus 2 to 4 inches, following the curves and contours. Smooth and ease the mat around curves, a few wrinkles will not matter. Tuck the edges of the mat under the large stones.

4 fill Use a bucket to fill the walkway area with gravel. Smooth and level the surface rock with the back side of the rake. Backfill behind the large stones with the soil removed to make the walk, covering any of the mat that shows beyond the large stones.

garden paths: stepping-stones

zones	time	skill
3–11	weekend	moderate

you will need

- 12-inch plastic dishpan or storage container
- rubber gloves
- builder's sand
- trowel
- masonry mix
- large plastic bucket
- objects as desired, such as shells, rocks, leaves, pieces of broken pottery, or tiles

making the mix

Plan to use about one gallon of ready-mix masonry for each 12-inch stone. In a large bucket, make a well in the center of the dry mixture; pour in about one quart of water. Blend until the mixture is the consistency of custard; add more water if needed. Wear rubber gloves while you mix the masonry. Use the mixture immediately.

footwork

right: **Crossing a lawn or traversing a garden bed, avoid leaving tracks in the grass or compacting the soil by marking the way with stepping-stones. Plain, unadorned stones are fine, but stones decorated with leaf impressions, shells, or other objects are particularly pretty. Use objects you have collected on vacations, flea market finds, leftover tiles, fern fronds, or large leaves.**

perennials

1 thyme, page 124

2 speedwell, page. 125

3 sedum, page. 123

4 daylily, page 115

5 bellflower, page 110

6 gooseneck loosestrife, page 118

7 garden phlox, page 120

1 mold Fill a plastic container with damp sand to within 2 inches of the top. Trowel the top level. Press leaves into place, vein side up. Or embed a mix of shells or objects in the sand; the side placed in the sand will be visible when the mixture dries.

2 mix Pour moistened masonry mix carefully into the mold without disturbing the objects. Trowel to settle the mixture, release air bubbles, and bring excess water to the surface. Do not dig into the sand or overtrowel. The surface should be level and smooth.

3 cure Cure the mold in the shade for 48 hours. Loosen the mold and invert onto plastic. Trowel off the excess sand, leaving some for texture. Hose off, and remove leaves with your fingers; some leaves may need to dry for 2 to 3 weeks in order to remove them.

4 place If you embedded objects in the mixture, hose off the excess sand; the objects will remain in the masonry. Set the stones on top of soil or mulch. To lay stones across a lawn, place the stones even with the soil surface so they do not interfere with mowing.

garden paths: a melange

dirt path

right: Firmly packed soil creates a path that blends in with the borders on each side. When you make the path, use a tamping tool to pack down the soil; subsequent foot traffic will keep it firm. Pitch the path to one side so water does not collect in the middle after rain. Weeds will have a difficult time germinating in the compacted soil, but you may want to run over it occasionally with a scuffle hoe to eliminate those that do grow.

planting pockets

below left: When laying a path, leave space between some of the stones or pavers to plant creeping or low-growing plants. You can plant a charming herb garden in this fashion; try the Mediterranean herbs—sage, rosemary, lavender, and oregano—that thrive in warmth and well-drained soil.

colorful stepping-stones

below right: For special spots in a garden bed, turn precast cement rounds into decorative art with pieces of broken tile and ceramic plates. Wear safety glasses while breaking up the material; and be careful handling the pieces because they have sharp edges. Use thin-set mortar to attach pieces to the round, and grout the spaces in between.

ever green

above: Grass, cut short, is a classic material for a path. Sod makes a neat walkway that is soft underfoot and its green hues set off the colors in the surrounding garden beds. Edge the path so the sod does not invade the beds—ordinary plastic or rubber edging is fine if you hide it by fronting it with courses of stone or brick or lengths of lumber.

woodland path

left: A gravel path blends in with this forestlike setting as it follows a sinuous trail through plantings of foxgloves, ajuga, ferns, and a towering climbing hydrangea. Keep the gravel from spilling into the borders with an edging of local stones or timber. In this kind of woodland design, pine needles and shredded bark would be equally suitable alternatives to the gravel.

fences for gardens

zones	exposure
3–8	sun or light shade

picking a style

Usually garden fences are part of the design of the bed or border. They are chosen more for their aesthetic appeal than privacy. If you want privacy and security, however, you can have an attractive surround. Board-on-board, grapestakes, woven boards, lath, bamboo, and chain link are just a few choices. Improve on chain link by planting vines to climb up and camouflage it. Wood fences have almost unlimited

classic pickets

right: A picket fence is surely one of the best and most traditional choices for showing off your garden. Painted white or left natural to weather to a silvery gray, a picket fence will mark boundaries without completely obstructing the view from either side. The pickets and posts can have plain, pointed, or rounded tops or fancy scrollwork and cutouts.

design and pattern possibilities.

Use a picket fence to enclose a part of the yard—around a cutting or vegetable garden, or an entry or foundation garden. Add a ready-made arbor over the gate for a clematis or a climbing rose.

basics

If you plan to build the fence yourself, check on zoning and permit requirements first.

All fences need sturdy support. With all but split rail, you should secure the posts in cement. You can sink posts for split rails directly into the soil.

perennials

1 daylily, page 115

2 lupine, page 118

3 rose campion, page 118

4 checkerbloom, page 123

5 chrysanthemum, page 111

6 iris, pages 130–131

other plants

a rose

b petunia

c chocolate mint

rustic country style

above: The friendly, open design of a split-rail fence borders a mixed planting of alliums, columbines, daisies, and foxgloves. The mortise-and-tenon fence will easily follow contours or zigzags.

victorian picket

right: A garden of delphiniums and poppies sparkles against the carved white pickets of this stylish fence. If you have a band saw, you can enjoy shaping the tops of the pickets yourself.

elegant wrought iron

left: Jackman clematis climbs, twines, and tumbles over an arbor and wrought-iron fence. Open fencing—with or without a gate—is the perfect support for other climbers as well, such as roses, morning glories, moonflowers, English and Boston ivy, and trumpet vine. Wrought-iron fencing is available prefabricated, which can make installation a do-it-yourself job. Wooden posts are usually set into concrete for stability.

modern openwork

below: To mark a boundary, with no thought of privacy, you can erect a framework of 2x4s with a gridwork of lattice. Such a fence is equally useful for climbing plants—even a wisteria, if you anchor the frame securely into the ground—and for delineating a bed in a flower or vegetable garden. The stepped design here adapts to level or sloping ground.

the
basics

getting started

begin with the soil

The success with gardening depends on the soil. This is especially true with perennials because they may remain in the same place for years. You need to improve the soil before planting. If you have good loam (not too much clay or sand), you should dig the area to a depth of 8 to 12 inches, removing large stones and weeds. Work compost into the top 3 to 4 inches.

fixing it up

If you have less than ideal soil, improve its tilth and moisture-holding ability by spreading a 2-inch layer of peat moss or compost on top of the soil and digging it in. Such amendments help sandy soil particles hold together and clay particles separate, so the former soil will release water more slowly and the latter will allow water to percolate through instead of collecting.

clay soil Soil with a lot of clay in it drains slowly but is high in nutrients. You can form a ball in your hand with clay soil; often the clay structure is not apparent until you have dug down 6 inches or more. If you think you could make bricks with your soil, it has a preponderance of clay.

loam The best soil type you can have is loam. It contains clay, sand, and silt in balanced proportions, along with humus. Humus, which is sometimes called black earth, is the result of decaying vegetable matter in the soil. It is fertile and makes up a good part of loam.

sandy soil Sandy soil is fine and porous. Water passes through this type of soil too easily. That is why it contains and holds few nutrients. The addition of peat moss will help the soil structure. Digging in aged manure and compost will raise its nutrient level.

1 prepare Lay out the shape of the garden bed with stakes and string to establish a pleasing shape and size. Slide a spade under the existing lawn to free it from the soil. If it is healthy turf, remove it in long segments, a spade-width across; roll it up as you remove it. Use the turf to patch areas of the lawn that might need attention.

2 amend Use a garden fork to break up the soil in the bed to a depth of at least 12 inches. Add at least 2 inches of organic matter (compost, leaf mold, well-rotted manure) to the exposed soil to improve its texture, drainage, and ability to retain moisture. Dig or fork it into the top 10 inches. This is the perfect time to add granular slow-acting fertilizer, if you wish.

3 rake Rake the soil smooth. Remove small stones. Break up clods or lumps of soil with the back of a steel rake. Make the bed as level as possible to ensure even distribution of rainwater.

add mulch

After you have planted your garden, spread a 3- to 4-inch layer of mulch over the soil. Use any mulch that is readily available, such as shredded fir bark, wood chips, compost, or seed hulls. (Cocoa bean hulls are fragrant, brown, attractive, and expensive; if you cannot resist them, use them in a small area, such as an herb garden, or top off a less expensive mulch with a thin layer of the hulls.)

Mulch helps the soil stay cool and retain moisture in hot weather. A thick layer also cuts down on weeds, preventing the seeds from germinating. You will find it easier to pull out weeds that germinate in the mulch (from seeds deposited courtesy of the wind or birds), because they will root in the loose mulch, not in the soil.

Mulch plants in late fall to protect them from the alternate freezing and thawing of the soil in winter.

planning & design

thinking ahead

right: Perennials, unlike annuals, do not bloom for months, or even a month, at a time. In deciding what to plant where, the plant's growth habit, foliage texture, shape, and season of bloom are as important as the colors of the flowers.

site selection

opposite top: If you plant a border or bed in full sun, you will have the largest choice of plants. Full sun means at least six hours of direct, unobstructed sun daily. In zones 8 to 11, most perennials appreciate some shade from the hot midday sun.

Place a garden anywhere—in front of a fence or hedge, by a patio or porch, along a walk or driveway, in the center of a lawn. For a country look, you might want to enclose it with a picket fence. For a formal look, surround it with a low-growing hedge, such as boxwood, or private, high-growing hedge of privet or yew.

color palettes

bottom left: Monochromatic gardens can be beautiful, but a garden of mixed colors can be far more interesting. Use contrast (blue fleabane with yellow coreopsis, for example) and harmony (pink poppies with rose coralbells) to create exciting combinations.

design pointers

below: Mix foliage types: spiky, feathery, strap-shape, grasslike, round, and heart-shape. A garden with only one type of foliage won't look as interesting, especially when the plants are not in bloom.

Use plants in odd-numbered groups and repeat the groups at intervals throughout the garden. A group is at least three plants of one variety. When using large plants, such as crambe or gunnera, one plant is sufficient.

When you plant a border, graduate heights from shortest at the edge to tallest in the rear, but be flexible. A few surprises lend variety. For example, a group of foxgloves in the middle or even at a front corner will appear to have seeded itself there (and it may have!). In a bed that is visible from all sides plant the tallest perennials in the center.

Use the aromatic plants. The most fragrant perennials include beebalm, bugbane, dames rocket, iris, peony, phlox, dianthus, and violets.

planting

starting out: year one

above: Even if you have drawn your garden design on paper—and you should have—you may want to make minor adjustments when you get the plants. Set the potted plants on top of the bed and rearrange them until you are sure you like the placement. Then unpot and plant them, spacing them according to their mature size. You can fill bare spots with annuals for the first year or two.

reaping the rewards: year two

right: Starting with nursery stock in large containers will give you a lush garden by the second year. Some plants, such as foxglove and hollyhock, are biennials, which produce foliage the first year, flowers the second. Others—sedum, phlox, peonies—require two to three years to reach their full blooming potential. Many will reseed, giving you an easy way to increase the colorful palette of your garden. If you start with small plants, continue to tuck annuals among them to fill the intervening spaces. Mulch well so that weeds do not have a chance to germinate on the bare soil.

1 unpot Prepare the soil and planting holes before you unpot the plants, so that the roots do not dry out. Water the pots one day prior to planting, to encourage as much soil as possible to cling to the root ball when you tap it out of the pot. A plant that has been growing in the pot too long will have roots encircling the soil, *left*.

2 tease When the plant is out of the pot, gently tease some of the roots, especially the bottom roots, away from the soil ball. If the pot holds multiple plants, use your fingers to separate the individual plants by gently pulling apart the roots.

Set the plants into the ground at the same depth or just slightly deeper than they were growing in the pot. Burying the crown (where stems meet roots) under too much soil can promote crown rot, which will kill the plant.

3 space Space plants at the distance their mature size will require. When you plant a groundcover, however, you may want to space the plants closer together for faster overall coverage. The usual method is to set out the plants in a W-shape pattern. Envision a plant at each of the points in the W. Set plants that increase by means of runners, such as pachysandra and sweet woodruff, slightly farther apart.

maintenance

1   **grooming** To keep the garden attractive all season, remove dead flowers and damaged, diseased, or dead foliage on a regular basis. A few perennials like daylilies, delphiniums, coralbells, and centaurea will produce additional flowering stems over a period of months if you are diligent about cutting off spent blooms. Do not compost diseased foliage; throw it into the trash.

You might want to leave some seedheads on plants to ripen. Collect the seeds (of species or open-pollinated perennials) to sow in the fall or the following spring. Leave the seedheads of asters, black-eyed Susans, coneflowers, and ornamental grasses; they provide food for birds in fall and winter.

2   **watering** Some watering devices are best used as garden ornaments. Old-fashioned sprinklers and fancy ones, such as this alligator, are best for watering the lawn or ornamenting the perennial garden. Most plants will be healthier if you do not wet the foliage. This is particularly true for phlox, beebalm, and other perennials that have a tendency to suffer from mildew.

3   **tip-top tools** Keep your tools in good shape. After each use, wipe off any soil that sticks to the head and dip the head into a bucket of sand to which you have added clean motor oil. Scour off rust with sandpaper. Put the tools in a designated space where they are kept clean and dry.

water wise No matter where you live, be conservative about water use. Water wisely with drip irrigation using a system of emitters, soaker hoses, or in-line sprinklers. The water gets right to the plants' roots instead of wasted through evaporation. Plants need at least 1 inch of water weekly from rain or from a hose.

winter protection Unless you live in a warm-winter zone, provide some protection from the cold and from the alternate freezing and thawing of the soil. You can use prunings from evergreen trees or a 3- to 4-inch layer of mulch, such as wood chips or straw. Wait until after the first hard freeze to apply winter mulch. Remove mulch gradually in spring as the air and soil warm. (The exception is early-blooming perennials, such as hellebores, Virginia bluebells, and Dutchman's breeches; pull back mulch from them in late winter or early spring.)

mulch Save time and effort when you weed and water by putting down a 3- to 4-inch layer of mulch, such as shredded wood or bark, in late spring. Weed seeds will not germinate readily without light; wind- or animal-borne weeds that appear are easy to pull up because they root in the mulch, not in the soil. The soil will retain moisture longer with a covering of mulch.

multiplying plants

why divide

There are many reasons for dividing plants (digging them up, separating them into sections, and then replanting) aside from the desire to have more of your favorites to spread around the garden. Although you can leave some perennials, such as peonies, undisturbed for decades, you will find that most plants benefit from being divided after spending three or more years in one place.

How do you know when you need to divide a plant? Look for these signs: The plant seems crowded, it produces fewer or smaller blooms than usual, or the center of the plant looks woody or browned.

Another reason for obtaining new plants by division instead of starting from seeds, cuttings, or layering is that division is easy to do and gives you plants that will usually bloom the same year.

dividing fibrous-rooted perennials

dig Before you divide a plant, dig the holes into which you will put the new divisions, so the roots will not dry out. With a garden spade, dig deep around and under the plant (a daylily, *right*), keeping as much of the root ball intact as possible.

divide Separate the clump into two or more sections (with roots) by slicing them apart with a sharp knife, cutting them with a spade (as with the coreopsis, *right*), or prying them apart with two garden forks placed back to back. Some perennials (sundrops, yarrow, and bugleweed, for example) produce rosettes from roots that grow around the edge of the plant; it is easy to cut off these rooted rosettes.

replant Remove dead or damaged roots from the division and cut back foliage by one-half to two-thirds. Plant immediately and water well. Some plants have special planting-depth requirements. Peonies, *right*, will not bloom or will take one to two years to flower if you set the roots deeper than 2 inches below the surface. Replant most perennials, however, at the same depth they were originally growing.

1 dividing iris

dig Dig up the crowded plants and wash off some of the dirt to expose new shoots and the rhizome to which they are attached. Break or cut apart the new rhizomes from the old clump.

2 divide Make sure each new rhizome has one or two leaf fans. Discard the oldest, woody rhizomes and any that show signs of disease or damage.

   Trim back the foliage by about two-thirds (to 5 inches) to compensate for the smaller number of roots. Before replanting, you can dip the rhizomes in sulfur powder to prevent mold.

3 plant Set the rhizomes 3 to 4 inches apart in shallow trenches, roots downward. Position them so all the leaf fans face the same direction (outward, or the direction in which you want them to grow). Cover the roots and about half of the rhizome with soil. Water well.

all in the timing

Divide most perennials in spring, just as new growth is beginning. If you live in the Deep South, divide in fall when the weather is cooler and wetter. It is easier to divide plants that do not have a lot of top growth. If they do, cut back the foliage by at least half, either before you dig them up or as you replant them.

   No matter what the zone, propagate peonies in late summer to fall, when their roots make the most growth. Divide iris in late summer, and spring-blooming perennials right after they have finished flowering.

   Some plants grow best (healthier and with excellent flower production) if they are divided them every one to two years. These include artemisia, New England aster, boltonia, chrysanthemum, Helen's flower, Joe-Pye weed, michaelmas daisy, primrose, black-eyed Susan, snow-in-summer, yarrow, and yellow loosestrife.

decorative ornaments

finishing touches

Ornaments direct visitors' attention to or away from an area. Decorative objects can camouflage the spareness of a new planting. They can be delightful surprises hidden among lush, mature perennials.

Artful plaques, small statues and even pyramid-shape piles of stones placed along the curve of a path can point the way to another garden bed.

Sculptures, obelisks, and fountains provide vertical accents in gardens that lack surrounding trees,

express yourself

right: Every garden is an expression of its owner's personality, from the shape and size of the bed to the colors of the plants and the design of paths and trellises. The ornaments you use to accent your perennial beds and borders are part of that expression, whether exuberant—like the playful items in this garden—or subtle.

trellises, walls, climbing vines, or other vertical components.

Select an item as a focal point instead of as an accent. Sundials, birdbaths, or even a bird feeder on a pole can easily be the center of attention in a garden. Any of these would be attractive in a country-style or naturalistic planting. For shade gardens, which tend to resemble woodlands, choose unobtrusive accents such as stonelike statues and wood sculpture.

Weather vanes and kinetic sculptures lend a sense of movement even when there is none; they are especially enjoyable on hot, windless summer days. As much as possible, select ornaments that you can leave in the garden year-round.

careful selection

below: **Choose decorative objects that complement the style of your garden. Cute rabbits or frogs, for instance, would look inappropriate in a formal garden edged with boxwood, whereas this gazing ball, a sundial, or armillary sphere are suitable.**

perennial gardens | **95**

display collections
above: Whatever your interest or hobby, indulge it to accent your garden, but do so with a bit of prudence.

fabulous finds
above right: A devotee of flea markets? Use your finds in unique ways, as in this hockey stick arbor.

flock with them
right: Love flamingos? Set them in a natural-looking group. Use their color to reflect the plantings—bleeding hearts and tulips.

special care

left: Although most ornaments sold for garden use are weatherproof, you will need to bring those that are not indoors to a basement or garage for winter in zones with freezing temperatures. Ceramic and concrete accessories may crack in temperatures below freezing. Others, like this statuesque crane, may be too fragile or valuable to be left outdoors to withstand the rigors of northern winters.

well-aged

below: Materials such as copper, iron, wood, and resin are, for the most part, impervious to rain and cold. The copper in the base of the sundial takes on a lovely shade of verdigris as it ages. Woods, such as redwood and cedar, turn silvery gray over the years.

seasonal checklist

	Spring	**Summer**

Cool Climates

Spring
- ☐ Begin to pull back winter mulch from perennial beds.
- ☐ Fertilize plants in beds and borders as new growth begins to emerge.
- ☐ Divide crowded or old clumps of summer- and fall-blooming perennials.
- ☐ Stake or support perennials that tend to get floppy before they grow too tall.
- ☐ Dig new garden beds; enlarge existing ones.
- ☐ Install drip irrigation.
- ☐ Set new plants into gardens. Water them thoroughly as soon as they are in place.
- ☐ Cut back flowering stems on bulbs as blooms fade; leave foliage to mature.

Summer
- ☐ Fill in vacant spots in the garden with annuals for continuous color.
- ☐ In early summer, divide perennials that bloomed in spring, except for iris and peonies. Divide those in late summer.
- ☐ Deadhead spent blooms to encourage more flowers later in the season.
- ☐ Mulch bare soil between plants to help retain moisture and prevent weeds.
- ☐ Inspect plants regularly for pests. Hose off aphids. Knock Japanese beetles into a jar of soapy water.
- ☐ Inspect plants for powdery mildew; spray regularly with an organic fungicide.
- ☐ Tuck errant stems of climbing vines into trellises, or prune them off.

Warm Climates

Spring
- ☐ Mulch bare soil between plants to help retain moisture and prevent weeds.
- ☐ Fill in vacant spots in the garden with annuals for continuous color.
- ☐ Install drip irrigation.
- ☐ Dig new garden beds; enlarge existing ones.
- ☐ Tuck errant stems of climbing vines into trellises, or prune them off.
- ☐ Inspect plants for pests. Hose off aphids. Knock Japanese beetles into a jar filled with soapy water.
- ☐ Plant container-grown perennials.

Summer
- ☐ Deadhead spent blooms to encourage more flowers later in the season.
- ☐ Water newly planted perennials regularly during dry spells.
- ☐ Divide bearded iris in late summer.
- ☐ Collect seeds of poppies, daylilies, and columbine to sow in fall.
- ☐ Inspect plants for powdery mildew; spray regularly with an organic fungicide.

Fall

☐ After a hard frost, cut back dead flower and foliage stems to within a few inches of the soil. Leave the plumes on ornamental grasses and the seedheads on coneflowers, black-eyed Susans, and other plants that provide food for winter birds.

☐ Plant new perennials such as peonies, chrysanthemums, and asters.

☐ Spread winter mulch over perennial beds after the ground freezes hard. Use several inches of straw, chopped leaves, or evergreen boughs.

☐ Build new compost bins or repair old ones. Turn and consolidate compost piles.

☐ Take a soil test while the ground is still workable.

☐ Plant spring-flowering bulbs for early color in perennial beds.

Winter

☐ If the ground hasn't frozen yet, finish planting bulbs that were overlooked during the fall.

☐ Make a list of perennials that will need dividing in spring.

☐ Look through mail-order catalogs and order plants for early- to late-spring arrival.

☐ Keep watering newly planted perennials as long as the ground is not frozen.

☐ After the holidays, cut up the Christmas tree and lay the boughs over any tender perennials.

☐ Plant pansies, calendulas, and primroses for fall and winter color.

☐ Deadhead and maintain the area around cool-season annuals such as larkspur.

☐ Divide overly large and overcrowded perennials to control size and promote next year's blooming.

☐ Plant new perennials.

☐ Cut back dead flower and foliage stems to within a few inches of the soil.

☐ Continue to remove weeds, especially perennial weeds.

☐ Keep lightweight fabric handy to cover and protect annuals from light frosts.

☐ Cut back chrysanthemums as they finish blooming; sidedress with fertilizer.

☐ Build new compost bins or repair old ones. Turn and consolidate compost piles to prepare for the new season.

☐ Prune and spray hybrid tea roses with dormant oil prior to leaf bud break. If leaves are out, use light (superior) oil.

☐ Protect perennials from heavy frost by covering them with a bed sheet, polyspun garden fabric, or a makeshift tent of plastic (with ventilation holes).

the
plants

common and botanical names

common name	botanical name
aeonium	*Aeonium* species
allium	*Allium* species and cultivars
artemisia	*Artemisia* species and cultivars
aster	*Aster* species and cultivars
astilbe	*Astilbe* × *arendsii*
aubretia	*Aubretia* × *deltoidea*
baby's breath	*Gypsophila paniculata*
balloon flower	*Platycodon grandiflorus*
bamboo	*Pleioblastus* species
baptisia	*Baptisia australis*
barrenwort	*Epimedium* species and cultivars
bearded iris	*Iris germanica*
beard-tongue	*Penstemon* species and cultivars
beebalm	*Monarda* species and cultivars
bellflower	*Campanula* species and cultivars
bergenia	*Bergenia ciliata*
black-eyed Susan	*Rudbeckia* species and cultivars
blazing star	*Liatris spicata*
bleeding heart	*Dicentra spectabilis*
blue false indigo	*Baptisia australis*
blue fescue	*Festuca glauca*
blue flag	*Iris versicolor*
blue oat grass	*Helictotrichon sempervirens*
blue star	*Amsonia tabernaemontana*
boltonia	*Boltonia asteroides*
bouncing bet	*Saponaria ocymoides*
bowles golden sedge	*Carex stricta* 'Bowles Golden'
brunnera	*Brunnera macrophylla*
butterfly weed	*Asclepias tuberosa*
candytuft	*Iberis sempervirens*
canterbury bells	*Campanula* species and cultivars
cardinal flower	*Lobelia cardinalis*
carolina lupine	*Thermopsis villosa*
catmint	*Nepeta* x *faassenii*
chamomile	*Chamaemelum nobile*
checkerbloom	*Sidalcea malviflora*
cholla	*Opuntia* species and cultivars
christmas fern	*Polystichum acrostichoides*
chrysanthemum	*Chrysanthemum* cultivars
cinnamon fern	*Osmunda cinnamomea*
clematis	*Clematis* species and cultivars
colewort	*Crambe cordifolia*
columbine	*Aquilegia* species and cultivars
coralbells	*Heuchera* species and cultivars
coreopsis	*Coreopsis* species and cultivars

common and botanical names

jupiter's beard	*Centranthus ruber*
kalimeris	*Kalimeris pinnatifida*
knautia	*Knautia macedonica*
lamb's ears	*Stachys byzantina*
lamium	*Lamium* species and cultivars
lavender cotton	*Santolina chamaecyparissus*
leopard plant	*Ligularia* species and cultivars
leopard's bane	*Doronicum caucasium*
lily	*Lilium* species and cultivars
lily-of-the-valley	*Convallaria majalis*
lilyturf	*Liriope* species and cultivars
louisiana iris	*Iris* hybrids
lungwort	*Pulmonaria* species and cultivars
lupine	*Lupinus* cultivars
maidenhair fern	*Adiantum pedatum*
marguerite	*Leucanthemum vulgare*
marsh marigold	*Caltha palustris*
meadow buttercup	*Ranunculus acris*
meadow rue	*Thalictrum* species and cultivars
mexican hat	*Ratibida columnifera*
milfoil	*Achillea* species and cultivars
miniature hollyhock	*Sidalcea malviflora*
monkshood	*Aconitum carmichaelii*
montbretia	*Crocosmia* species and cultivars
moss phlox	*Phlox subulata*
mountain pink	*Phlox subulata*
mugwort	*Artemisia* species and cultivars
mullein	*Verbascum* species and cultivars
navelwort	*Omphaloides cappadocica*
omphaloides	*Omphaloides cappadocica*
oriental poppy	*Papaver orientale*
orris	*Iris pallida*
ostrich fern	*Matteuccia struthiopteris*
ox-eye daisy	*Leucanthemum vulgare*
pampas grass	*Cortaderia selloana*
peony	*Paeonia lactiflora* and cultivars
periwinkle	*Vinca minor*
pinks	*Dianthus* species and cultivars
prairie coneflower	*Ratibida columnifera*
prickly pear	*Opuntia* species and cultivars
primrose	*Primula* species and cultivars
pulmonaria	*Pulmonaria* species and cultivars
purple coneflower	*Echinacea purpurea*
queen-of-the-prairie	*Filipendula rubra*
red hot poker	*Kniphofia* species and cultivars
red valerian	*Centranthus ruber*

Achillea species and cultivars
yarrow (milfoil)
2'–4' tall
Pink, rose, red, white, pale yellow blooms
Flowers summer to fall
Sun
Zones 3–9
Use in border, butterfly, container, or cutting
gardens

Feathery, grayish green foliage and flat-topped clusters of flowers add texture and airy accents to borders. Easy to grow; needs good drainage; drought-tolerant.

Aconitum carmichaelii
monkshood
3'–6' tall
Deep blue to purple blooms
Flowers mid- to late summer
Partial sun to light shade
Zones 4–8
Use in border gardens

Desirable for its deep color in late summer. Deeply cut leaves are attractive all season. All parts of the plant, including the blossoms, are *very* poisonous; **do not plant if you have curious young children.**

Aeonium species
aeonium
6"–10" tall
Yellow, white, red blooms
Flowers spring
Sun
Zones 9–11
Use in border, container, and Xeriscape
gardens

Much appreciated for its rosettes of leaves. Use as a specimen planting or mix with other plants. 'Zwartkopf' with its deep burgundy leaves makes a bold garden statement.

perennial plants

Aethionema armenum
stone cress
8"–12" tall
Pink, white blooms
Flowers late spring
Sun
Zones 6–9
Use in border, container, and rock gardens

Tufts of grayish green leaves covered with flowers in spring. Needs good drainage. Shear after blooms fade to keep looking neat. 'Warley Rose' is a beautiful interspecific cross with blue-gray leaves tinted red, and dark pink flowers striped with light pink veins.

Alcea rosea
hollyhock
4'–8' tall
Pink, rose, red, purple, white, pale yellow blooms
Flowers summer to late summer
Sun
Zones 3–9
Use in border gardens

Wonderfully showy, old–fashioned plant for the back of the border. Single- and double-flowered cultivars available: Powderpuff Hybrids, 'Chater's Double'. Actually a biennial that self-seeds, so seems perennial. Not long-lived. Transplant seedlings in spring.

Allium species
allium (flowering onion)
1'–3' tall
Fragrant pink, lilac, blue, yellow, white blooms
Flowers late spring to early summer
Sun
Zones 4–9
Use in border, container, cutting, and edible
gardens

Hundreds of species, including chives (*A. schoenoprasum*), which look as good edging a border as they do in an herb garden. Other ornamental alliums range from petite, yellow *A. moly* to lilac-blue *A. christophii*, with its gigantic globular flower, and rosy purple *A. pulchellum*, which has loose, pendulous florets. Alliums may self-sow but not invasively.

Amsonia tabernaemontana
blue star (willow amsonia)
2'–3' tall
Slate blue blooms
Flowers late spring to early summer
Sun to light shade
Zones 5–9
Use in border and naturalistic gardens

Native to North America. Star-shape flowers add sparkle to lightly shaded gardens. Easy to grow; self-sows prolifically. Combines well with coreopsis, blue false indigo, iris, and low-growing phlox.

Armeria maritima
sea pink (thrift)
4"–10" tall
Pink, red, white blooms
Flowers late spring to early summer
Sun
Zones 3–9
Use in border, rock, and wild gardens

Grassy leaves and bright flowers. Good as an edging at the front of a border or popping up among rocks. Good groundcover. Attracts hummingbirds. Easy to grow. 'Alba' is white.

Anemone blanda
greek windflower
6" tall
Blue, mauve, pink, white blooms
Flowers spring
Light shade
Zones 5–8
Use in border, container, and wild gardens, and as a groundcover

Delightful, daisy-like flowers and divided leaves. Creates a carpet of color under deciduous trees. Easy to grow. Spreads slowly in soil with good drainage. Does not require division, although that is a good way to increase the plants. There are many cultivars.

Artemisia species and cultivars
artemisia (mugwort)
1'–2' tall
Silver-gray; fragrant leaves; insignificant blooms
Flowers summer
Sun
Zones 4–9
Use in border, container, and cutting gardens and as a groundcover

Beautiful, feathery foliage plant for midborder. Some are native to North America. Spreads, sometimes aggressively, by underground runners. 'Silver Mound' is more restrained than 'Silver King' and 'Silver Queen'.

Aquilegia species and cultivars
columbine
1½'–2' tall
Red, blue, yellow, white, and bicolor blooms
Flowers late spring to early summer
Sun
Zones 3–9
Use in border, container, and wild gardens

Native to North America. Large-flowered McKana Hybrids and compact and long-spurred Music Hybrids are excellent strains. Graceful plants for the front of borders. Not long-lived but self-sows freely.

Arum italicum 'Pictum'
variegated italian arum
12"–18" tall
Greenish yellow- or white-margined leaves; purple blooms
Flowers late spring to early summer
Partial sun to light shade
Zones 4–9
Use in shade gardens, and as a groundcover

Dark green marbled foliage appears in fall, persists through winter, disappears in late spring. Clusters of orange-red berries last for weeks. Combines well with creeping phlox.

107

Aruncus dioicus
goatsbeard
3'–4½' tall
White, cream blooms with unpleasant fragrance
Flowers late spring to summer
Sun to light shade
Zones 6–9
Use in borders and wild gardens

An imposing plant because of its size. Feathery, 12-inch-long plumes lend an airy aspect. Good at rear of borders or near trees. Combines well with ornamental grasses.

Asarum canadense
wild ginger
5"–8" tall
Purple-brown, inconspicuous blooms
Flowers spring
Light shade to shade
Zones 4–8
Use in naturalistic gardens, and as a groundcover

Native to North America. Deciduous heart-shape leaves. Other species are evergreen—*A. virginicum* (hardy to Zone 7), *A. europaeum* European ginger (hardy to Zone 5). Combines well with sweet woodruff, hellebore, and epimedium.

Asclepias tuberosa
butterfly weed
2'–3' tall
Fragrant orange, yellow, pink, vermilion blooms
Flowers summer
Sun
Zones 3–9
Use in border, butterfly, and container gardens

A must-have native that attracts butterflies. Drought-tolerant. Slow to emerge in spring; be careful not to dig up the roots. Colorful flower clusters. Easy to grow; pest- and disease-free.

perennial plants

Aster species and cultivars
aster
2' tall
Blue blooms
Flowers late summer to fall
Sun
Zones 4–9
Use in border, butterfly, and wild gardens

Very long-blooming. Another excellent cultivar is 'Wonder of Staffa' (lavender-blue). *A. novae-angliae* (New England aster) and *A. novi-belgii* (Michaelmas daisy) are native to North America, with scores of cultivars and colors from white and pink to red and claret.

Astilbe x *arendsii*
astilbe (false goatsbeard)
2'–3' tall
Pink, rose, red, white blooms
Flowers early summer
Partial sun to shade
Zones 5–8
Use in border, container, and cutting gardens

Finely divided foliage makes plant attractive even without its flowers. Does not grow well in areas with hot, humid summers. Combines well with hostas, hellebores, and ferns.

Aubretia x *deltoidea*
aubretia
6"–9" tall
Mauve, magenta, rose, pink, white blooms
Flowers late spring
Sun to light shade
Zones 4–8
Use in border, container, and rock gardens;
     and as a groundcover

Mat-forming evergreen plant with long-lasting single or double blooms. Prefers sandy soil, good drainage. Cut off spent blooms to keep plant compact. Hybrids include 'Borsch's White', 'Purple Gem', and *A. deltoidea* 'Variegata' (blue flowers, silvery white-edged foliage).

Baptisia australis
baptisia (blue false indigo)
2'–3' tall
Deep blue blooms
Flowers late spring to summer
Sun
Zones 4–8
Use in border and naturalistic gardens

Lupine-like flowers. There are several species that bear white blossoms. *Baptisia lactea* blooms in spring and *B. leucantha* is hardy to Zone 3. *B. tinctoria* is a yellow-flowered species.

Boltonia asteroides
boltonia
4'–5' tall
White, pink, purple, violet blooms
Flowers late summer
Sun
Zones 3–9
Use in border and cutting gardens

White-flowered 'Snowbank' is a lovely, vigorous cultivar. 'Nana' (a cultivar of *B.* var. *latisquama*, a southeastern American native plant) is 3 feet tall. Combines well with fountain grass, asters, and Russian sage.

Begonia grandis
hardy begonia
1½'–2½' tall
Fragrant pink blooms
Flowers summer
Partial sun to light shade
Zones 7–10
Use in borders, containers, and as a groundcover

Angel-wing-shape leaves are red beneath; reddish stems. Forms bulblets in leaf axils; keep them in dry peat moss over winter and plant in spring. 'Alba' has white flowers. Adds a charming, light touch to the garden.

Brunnera macrophylla
brunnera (siberian bugloss)
8"–18" tall
Bright blue blooms
Flowers late spring
Light shade
Zones 3–9
Use in borders and as a groundcover

Forget-me-not-like flowers. With sufficient moisture, grows in sun as well as shade. Easy to grow. Variegated cultivars ('Hadspen Cream' and 'Variegata') need protection from sun and wind to prevent burning. Self-seeds freely.

Bergenia ciliata
bergenia
10"–20" tall
Rose, pink, red, white blooms
Flowers midspring
Light shade
Zones 3–9
Use in borders and as a groundcover

Evergreen, usually heart-shape leaves. Prefers moist soil; tolerates dry. Green or burgundy foliage. White blooms of 'Silberlicht' ('Silver Light') become tinted pink as they age.

Caltha palustris
marsh marigold
18" tall
Fragrant yellow blooms
Flowers spring
Light shade
Zones 4–10
Use in border, edible, and naturalistic gardens

Prefers moist sites, near a pond, for example. There are double- and white-flowered forms. Dies to the ground in summer; tuck it where other plants will cover the empty space. Leaves are edible when cooked like spinach.

Campanula species and cultivars
bellflower (harebell, canterbury bells)
6"–48" tall
Blue, white blooms
Flowers summer
Sun to light shade
Zones 3–9
Use in border, container, cutting, and rock gardens

From small *C. carpatica* to medium *C. glomerata* and tall *C. latifolia*, bellflowers are showy, easy-care plants. There are many cultivars to suit any color scheme in the blue to white range.

Campsis radicans
trumpet vine
15'–20' tall
Orange, red, yellow blooms
Flowers summer to fall
Sun
Zones 4–10
Use on trellises, arbors; attracts hummingbirds

Native to southeastern North America. Climbs quickly by aerial roots. Very heat- and drought-tolerant. 'Crimson Trumpet' and 'Praecox' have large red blooms; 'Flava', yellow flowers; 'Mme. Galen', apricot.

Centranthus ruber
red valerian (jupiter's beard)
30"–36" tall
Very fragrant crimson to rose blooms
Flowers early to late summer
Sun or light shade
Zones 4–9
Use in border, butterfly, container, and cutting gardens

Easy to grow; readily self-seeds. Shear after flowering to encourage rebloom. Drought-tolerant, but water helps keep the plant from getting woody. 'Albus' has white flowers.

perennial plants

Cerastium tomentosum
snow–in–summer
6"–12" tall
White blooms
Flowers early summer
Sun to light shade
Zones 3–8
Use in container and rock gardens, and as a groundcover

Silvery gray leaves and pure white flowers are eye-catching. Easy to grow; can be invasive; 'Silver Carpet' and 'Yo-Yo' are less so. Shear off spent blooms to keep plant looking neat.

Chamaemelum nobile (Anthemis nobile)
chamomile
8"–12" tall
Fragrant white daisylike blooms
Flowers late spring through summer
Sun to light shade
Zones 6–9
Use in border and container gardens

Herb with apple-scented flowers on slender stalks. After flowers fade, shear back to encourage reblooming. Used in teas and tisanes. May cause contact dermatitis in susceptible people.

Chelone glabra
turtlehead
2'–3' tall
Rose–white, purple blooms
Flowers mid- to late summer
Sun to light shade
Zones 3–9
Use in borders

Native to North America. Easy to grow in moist soil. Stiff stems make it quite weather-resistant. Related species bloom later, into September including rosy purple *C. obliqua* and pink *C. lyonii*, which cannot take full sun, especially in warm zones.

Chrysanthemum (Dendranthema) cultivars
chrysanthemum
1'–3' tall
All colors (except blue) and bicolor blooms
Flowers late summer through fall
Sun
Zones 4–9
Use in border, container, and cutting gardens

Traditional fall flower. Easy care. Does best when divided every year; discard the older center clump. Flowers vary in size and shape, from small buttons to large dahlia types. Scores of cultivars are available.

Coreopsis species and cultivars
coreopsis (tickseed)
1½'–2½' tall
Bright to pale yellow blooms
Flowers early to midsummer
Sun to light shade
Zones 3–9
Use in border, butterfly, container, and cutting gardens

Dependable, long-blooming native perennial. Single- and double-flowered cultivars. Deadhead for continued flowering. Combines well with any other perennials.

Clematis species and cultivars
clematis
5"–12' tall
Blue, white, pink, purple, red, and bicolor blooms; some are fragrant
Flowers summer to fall
Sun
Zones 3–9, depending on species
Use as a vine for trellises and arbors

Wonderful on an arbor alone or with climbing roses. Fluffy seed heads add long-season interest. The many species and cultivars vary in season of bloom and in height. Plant with roots in shade, tops in sun.

Corydalis lutea
corydalis
9"–12" tall
Yellow blooms
Flowers early spring to late summer
Partial sun to light shade
Zones 5–8
Use in border, rock, and naturalistic gardens

Small flowers resemble those of its relative, bleeding heart. Self-sows readily. Will grow in rock walls and between paving stones as well as at the front of a border. 'Alba' has white flowers. Not bothered by pests or diseases; does not transplant easily.

Convallaria majalis
lily–of–the–valley
6"–8" tall
Fragrant white, pink blooms
Flowers mid- to late spring
Partial sun to shade
Zones 2–9
Use in naturalistic gardens, and as a groundcover

Wonderful, sweet fragrance. Tolerates dry soil but prefers rich, moist soil; competes well with shallow tree roots. Spreads slowly. Combines well with deciduous trees and shrubs.

Crambe cordifolia
crambe (colewort)
2'–6' tall
Fragrant white blooms
Flowers early summer
Sun
Zones 6–9
Use in border gardens, and as a specimen plant

The immense heart-shape leaves are magnificent at the rear of a border in a large garden. Stake the flower stalks. Slugs may be a problem; otherwise, an easy plant to grow if given a lot of space. Birds like the seeds.

Crocosmia cultivars
montbretia

3'–3½' tall
Fragrant flame red, yellow, orange, apricot blooms
Flowers midsummer
Sun to light shade
Zones 6–9
Use in border, container, cutting, naturalistic, and hummingbird gardens

One of the better-known cultivars is 'Lucifer', a bigeneric hybrid with flowers that last 3 to 4 weeks. Needs well-drained soil. Mulch well for winter in the North.

Cyclamen hederifolium (C. neapolitanum)
hardy cyclamen

3"–4" tall
Fragrant white with crimson eye or pink blooms
Flowers fall
Light shade to medium shade
Zones 6–8
Use in border, container, hillside, and naturalistic gardens

Heart-shape green leaves mottled with silver appear in fall, last through winter, disappear in spring. Leave the plant undisturbed for years; it will spread slowly. Easy to grow in soil with good drainage.

Delosperma cooperi
hardy iceplant

2"–4" tall
Purple–red blooms
Flowers summer to fall
Sun
Zones 6–9
Use in border, Xeriscape, and container gardens, and as a groundcover

Showy plant for Xeriscape gardens. Spreads but not invasively. Requires soil with good drainage. Pest- and disease-free. One of the truly low-maintenance plants. Combines well with cacti and succulents.

perennial plants

Delphinium cultivars
delphinium

3'–6' tall
Fragrant blue, white, pink blooms
Flowers early to midsummer
Sun to light shade
Zones 3–8
Use in border and cutting gardens

Stately, back-of-the-border plant; not long-lived. Stake tall flower stalks; cut back spent stalks for rebloom. Needs alkaline soil. Grows best in cool climates. May be bothered by mildew, black spot, mites, and slugs. Cultivars of the 'Pacific Hybrid' strain are noteworthy.

Dianthus species and cultivars
dianthus (pinks)

6"–18" tall
Fragrant pink, rose, red, and white blooms
Flowers late spring to midsummer
Sun to light shade
Zones 4–9
Use in border and cutting gardens

Old-fashioned perennial for the front of a border. Newer cultivars will often rebloom until September if you deadhead spent flowers. Many have evergreen foliage. Provide winter protection in cold zones with a layer of mulch. Cultivars include spring-blooming 'Bath's Pink' (blue-green foliage), everblooming 'Zing Rose', and deep red 'Desmond'.

Dicentra spectabilis
bleeding heart

12"–20" tall
Pink, white blooms
Flowers late spring to early summer
Light shade
Zones 3–9
Use in borders and cutting gardens

Lovely plant for the shade garden. Goes dormant by midsummer; plant with hosta, ferns, and astilbes to disguise the empty space. 'Alba' is a white-flowered cultivar. The foliage of *D. eximia* and *D. formosa* does not die down in summer. Dutchman's breeches, *D. cucullaria*, bears white blooms in early spring.

Dictamnus albus
gas plant (dittany)
2'–4' tall
Fragrant dark purple, pink, white blooms
Flowers early to midsummer
Sun to light shade
Zones 3–8
Use in border gardens

Fairly drought-tolerant. Leaves have a lemon fragrance when crushed (foliage can cause dermatitis; seeds are toxic). 'Purpureus' has mauve blooms; 'Rubra', rosy purple blooms.

Echinacea purpurea
purple coneflower
3'–4' tall
Dark pink blooms with brownish-purple disk
Flowers summer to fall
Sun
Zones 3–9
Use in border, bird, butterfly, container, and
    cutting gardens

Native eastern North American plant. Attracts wildlife. Long bloom season. Drought-tolerant. Many cultivars: purple 'Magnus', pink 'Crimson Star', 18-inch-tall 'White Swan'.

Digitalis purpurea
foxglove
2'–4' tall
Pink, white, purple-spotted blooms
Flowers early to midsummer
Partial sun to light shade
Zones 4–8
Use in border and cutting gardens

Classic plant for the rear of a border. Perfect for a cottage garden. Not long-lived (usually biennial) but self-sows freely. Cut off spent flower stems for a second blooming. The 'Excelsior' and 'Shirley' strains have blooms all around the stem, not just on one side. *D. grandiflora* and *D. lutea* have yellow blooms.

Epimedium species and cultivars
epimedium (barrenwort)
4"–12" tall
Pink, yellow, violet, crimson, white blooms
Flowers spring
Light shade
Zones 4–8
Use as a groundcover

Heart-shape foliage, often evergreen, is veined red as it emerges in spring. Hardly ever needs dividing. Very easy to grow. Spurred flowers are bicolored except in white and yellow cultivars.

Doronicum caucasium
leopard's bane
18"–24" tall
Yellow blooms
Flowers early spring
Sun to partial shade
Zones 3–8
Use in border and woodland gardens

Prefers humusy, well-drained soil. Handsome heart- to kidney-shape leaves near ground level; daisy-like flowers rise above them. Ephemeral perennial that disappears in hot weather. Good companion for spring bulbs.

Eupatorium maculatum
joe–pye weed
6'–10' tall
Rosy purple, wine-red blooms
Flowers late summer
Sun to light shade
Zones 3–8
Use in border, butterfly, cutting, and
    naturalistic gardens

North American native. Very easy to grow. Suitable for back of a border. Combine with ornamental grasses, asters, and goldenrod. 'Atropurpureum' has purple-tinted foliage.

Euphorbia polychroma (E. epithymoides)
cushion spurge

8"–10" tall
Chartreuse and bright yellow blooms
Flowers spring
Sun to light shade
Zones 6–11
Use in border, container, and Xeriscape
gardens, and as a groundcover

Clump-forming; leaves, sometimes tinged
purple, turn deep red in fall. Clusters of tiny
flowers. Undemanding, self-sows freely. Myrtle
spurge (*E. myrsinites*) is hardy from zones 5 to 8.

Filipendula rubra
queen–of–the–prairie

5'–9' tall
Slightly fragrant, pink, deep rose blooms
Flowers early to midsummer
Light shade
Zones 3–9
Use in border, naturalistic, and butterfly
gardens

North American native. Prefers moist, rich soil.
Striking at the rear of a border with its large,
deep green, divided leaves and fluffy plumes.
Doesn't need staking. Combines well with
Japanese iris. 'Venusta' has deep rose flowers.

Galium odoratum
sweet woodruff

6"–8" tall
White blooms; fragrant foliage
Flowers late spring to early summer
Light shade
Zones 4–8
Use as a groundcover

Scent of stems, especially when dried, is
reminiscent of new-mown hay. In centuries
past, sweet woodruff was strewn on the floor
to scent a room. Combines well with other
shade-loving perennials, such as hostas and
ferns. Prefers moist soil.

perennial plants

Geranium species and cultivars
cranesbill

4"–24" tall
Blue, pink, purple, rose, red, white blooms
Flowers late spring to summer or fall
Sun to light shade
Zones 5–9
Use in border, container, rock, and
naturalistic gardens and as groundcover

Lovely at the front of a border. Avoid
afternoon sun in hot zones. Excellent cultivars
include 'Johnson's Blue', 'Wargrave Pink', and
'Striatum'. Combines well with dianthus, hosta,
blue oat grass, and other ornamental grasses.

Gypsophila paniculata
baby's breath

2'–3' tall
White, pink blooms
Flowers summer
Sun
Zones 3–8
Use in border and cutting gardens

Creates a delicate, airy filler in the garden.
Combines well with roses, cranesbill, lavender,
and salvias. 'Bristol Fairy' has double white
blooms; 'Pink Fairy' is smaller, growing to
1½ to 2 feet tall, with double pink flowers. Cut
back after first flush of bloom for a second
flowering. May need staking. Flowers can be
used fresh or dried in arrangements.

Hedera species and cultivars
ivy

20'–50' tall
No flowers
Sun to shade
Zones 4–9
Use as a vine for containers, as a groundcover,
or in a cutting garden

English ivy (*H. helix*) is best known. Aggressive
and invasive; it can disguise a fence in 2 to
3 years. Cultivars include 'Glacier', with foliage
splotched white, slower-growing 'Needlepoint'
with very small leaves. Plants that die back
to the ground in winter may revive from the
roots in spring. Prune to control spread.

Helianthemum species and cultivars
rock rose (sun rose)
9"–18" tall
Yellow, apricot, crimson, pink blooms
Flowers early summer
Sun
Zones 5–9
Use in border, rock, and Xeriscape gardens
   and as groundcover

Sprawling plant with gray-green leaves.
Provide protective mulch in cold-winter areas.
Easy care but may be short-lived. Cut back
after bloom for second flowering in fall.
'Raspberry Ripples' is a good cultivar.

Hemerocallis species and cultivars
daylily
1'–3' tall
All colors (no blue); bicolor blooms, some fragrant
Flowers early to late summer;
Sun to light shade
Zones 4–9
Use in border, butterfly, and cutting gardens
   and as a groundcover

One of the easiest to grow (and most hybridized)
of all perennials. Usually each flower lasts only a
day. Tolerates drought when not in bloom. Some
are evergreen in warm zones. Look for tetraploids.

Heliopsis helianthoides
false sunflower
30"–60" tall
Yellow, gold blooms
Flowers summer to fall
Sun
Zones 4–9
Use in border, cutting, naturalistic, and
   Xeriscape gardens

Native to North America. Brightly colored,
daisylike flowers. Does not need staking. Single
or double blooms. 'Loraine Sunshine' has
white leaves variegated with green
veins. Combines well with asters, Shasta
daisy, garden phlox, and speedwell.

Heuchera sanguinea
coralbells
18"–24" tall
Pink, white, rose, red blooms
Flowers late spring to late summer
Sun to light shade
Zones 3–9
Use in border, butterfly, cutting, and rock
   gardens, and as a groundcover

Native to North America. Grown as much for
its evergreen foliage as its flowers. Ruffled
leaves often purple-bronze ('Palace Purple'),
marbled silver ('Frosty'), or variegated cream.
For rebloom, cut off spent flower stems. Long-
lived. Provide winter mulch in northern zones.

Helleborus species and cultivars
hellebore
12"–18" tall
Green, white, cream, mauve, rose, pink blooms
Flowers late winter to early spring
Light shade
Zones 5–8
Use in border, cutting, and naturalistic
   gardens, and as a groundcover

Color when virtually nothing else is in bloom:
H. niger, Christmas rose, flowers January to
March; *H. orientalis*, Lenten rose, blooms March
to mid-May. Many hybrids between the two.
Dislikes heat and transplanting.

Hibiscus moscheutos
rose mallow (swamp rose mallow)
3'–4' tall
Light and deep pink, rose, white blooms
Flowers late spring to summer
Sun to light shade
Zones 5–9
Use in border, container, and cutting gardens

Native to southern North America. Huge
blooms are striking in the garden. Prefers
moist, well-drained soil. Excellent cultivars
include magenta pink 'Ann Arundel',
'White Giant', and crimson 'Southern Belle'.

Hosta species and cultivars
hosta
6"–36" tall
Lavender, blue, white blooms, some fragrant
Flowers summer
Partial sun to shade
Zones 3–9
Use in border, containers, and as groundcover

Excellent foliage plant for shade gardens. Slender, lance-shape, heart-shape, or rounded leaves in chartreuse, green, or blue, often variegated or edged in white or gold. May be bothered by slugs or black vine weevils.

Iberis sempervirens
candytuft
9"–12" tall
White blooms
Flowers spring
Sun
Zones 4–8
Use in border and rock gardens

Evergreen foliage attractive year-round. Easy to grow, not troubled by pests or diseases. Shear after flowering to keep plants compact. Combines well with spring-flowering bulbs. There are many cultivars. 'Autumn Beauty' and 'Autumn Snow' rebloom in fall.

Jasione laevis (J. perennis)
sheep's bit
5"–18" tall
Blue blooms
Flowers summer
Sun to light shade
Zones 5–9
Use in border, cutting, and rock gardens

Same family as bellflowers. Not often grown but makes a lovely border edging. Produces flowers, which resemble those of scabiosa, throughout summer. Prefers sandy soil. 'Blue Light' has vivid blue flowers on 2-foot stems.

perennial plants

Kalimeris pinnatifida
kalimeris
2'–3' tall
White, red blooms
Flowers summer to fall
Sun
Zones 5–9
Use in border, butterfly, and cutting gardens

Formerly known as *Boltonia cantoniensis*, kalimeris combines well with boltonia as well as asters, goldenrod, chrysanthemums, and ornamental grasses. Doesn't need staking. The species has white blooms, which help soften dramatic color contrasts.

Kirengeshoma palmata
yellowbells
3'–4' tall
Pale yellow blooms
Flowers late summer to early fall
Partial sun to light shade
Zones 5–9
Use in border and naturalistic gardens

Graceful plant that resembles a shrub with its deciduous, maple-shape leaves on reddish purple stems. Makes an excellent specimen plant in moist but well-drained soil.

Knautia macedonica
knautia
18"–24" tall
Wine red blooms
Flowers summer to fall
Sun
Zones 5–9
Use in border, cutting, and naturalistic gardens

Tall, slender, lax stems weave among other perennials and ornamental grasses. Self-sows freely but not invasively; seedlings are easy to pull up in spring and transplant or discard. Prefers well-drained soil.

Kniphofia species and cultivars
red hot poker (torchlily)
18"–60" tall
Flame red, orange, cream, pink, yellow blooms
Flowers summer to fall
Sun
Zones 6–10
Use in border, container, cutting, and
   naturalistic gardens

Stunning plant for the border. A tender
perennial in cold zones; mulch well or dig up
and store roots for winter. Scores of cultivars.

Liatris spicata
gayfeather (blazing star)
2'–3' tall
Reddish purple, white, blue, violet blooms
Flowers summer to fall
Sun to light shade
Zones 3–10
Use in border, butterfly, cutting, and
   naturalistic gardens

Native to North America. Flowers open from
the top down. Easy to grow; no pests or
diseases. Prefers moist, well-drained soil. Cut
flowers are long-lasting, as is the plant itself.

Lamium species and cultivars
lamium (dead nettle)
12"–18" tall
Pink, white, purple, yellow blooms
Flowers late spring to summer
Light shade to full shade
Zones 3–10
Use in border and container gardens, and as a
   groundcover

Can be invasive; easy to grow; tolerant of dry
shade. Shear after flowering; foliage has all-
season appeal, often variegated or brushed with
silver or pale green. 'Beacon Silver' has silver
leaves edged in green, pink blooms; grows to 8
inches. 'Pink Pewter' (shown) is deeper pink.

Ligularia species and cultivars
leopard plant
24"–30" tall
Fragrant bright orange, yellow blooms
Flowers mid- to late summer
Partial sun to light shade
Zones 4–9
Use in border, container, and naturalistic
   gardens

Wonderful for its serrated, round, or arrow-
pointed foliage all season; leaves of some
cultivars are purple ('Desdemona', 'Othello').
L. stenocephala 'The Rocket' reaches 4 feet in
height. Needs constantly moist soil to flourish.
Mulch for winter protection in cold zones.

Leucanthemum vulgare
ox-eye daisy (marguerite)
15"–36" tall
White blooms with yellow centers
Flowers late spring to early summer
Sun to light shade
Zones 5–9
Use in border, butterfly, and cutting gardens

Easy to grow in constantly moist but well-
drained soil. Deadhead for continuous bloom.
Related to Shasta daisy, which has many
cultivars with single, semidouble, and double
flowers, including 'Snowcap' and 'Agalia'.

Lilium species and cultivars
lily
2'–7' tall
Fragrant white, pink, red, maroon, yellow,
   orange, and bicolor blooms
Flowers early to late summer
Sun
Zones 4–8
Use in border, container, and cutting gardens

From Asiatic hybrids flowering in June to
Oriental hybrids in August and species in
between and beyond, there is a lily for every
garden. Many species are native to North
America. Easy to grow; requires good
drainage; tall cultivars may need staking.

Liriope species and cultivars
lilyturf
12"–15" tall
Dark mauve, lilac, white blooms
Flowers late summer to early fall
Sun
Zones 6–10
Use in border, cutting, and naturalistic gardens

Evergreen, arching, grasslike foliage. Cut back old foliage in early spring. Leaves may be variegated white or yellow. Cultivars include yellow-striped 'Variegata', large-flowered 'Monroe White', and rich violet 'Majestic'.

Lobelia cardinalis
cardinal flower
2'–4' tall
Scarlet, white, pink blooms
Flowers mid to late summer
Sun to light shade
Zones 2–9
Use in border, butterfly, hummingbird, and naturalistic gardens

Native to North America. Usually short-lived but self-sows freely. Prefers constantly moist soil. 'Alba' has white blooms; 'Rosea', pink.

Lupinus Russell Hybrids
lupine
3'–4' tall
Pink, red, blue, yellow, white, bicolor blooms
Flowers late spring to summer
Sun to light shade
Zones 4–7
Use in border, cutting, butterfly, and naturalistic gardens

Prefers cool, evenly moist, acid soil. Challenging to grow and worth it when it blooms en masse in midborder. Reseeds. Cut off spent flower stalks to promote rebloom. Attractive foliage. Combines well with Siberian iris and salvias.

perennial plants

Lychnis coronaria
rose campion
1'–2' tall
Cerise blooms
Flowers early summer
Full to partial sun
Zones 3–9
Use in border, container, naturalistic, and cutting gardens, and as a groundcover

Grayish white, hairy leaves; stems bear small, solitary flowers. Short-lived but reseeds freely. Easy to grow in any soil; will survive in parts of Zone 9 where humidity is not high. 'Alba' has white flowers; 'Ocellata', white with a bright pink eye; 'Flore Pleno' is double-flowered.

Lysimachia punctata
yellow loosestrife
2'–3' tall
Bright yellow blooms
Flowers early to late summer
Sun to light shade
Zones 4–9
Use in border, butterfly, and naturalistic gardens, and as a groundcover

Tall with upright whorls of yellow blooms. Old-fashioned, easy to grow. Can spread invasively. Gooseneck loosestrife (*Lysimachia clethroides*) grows about 2½ feet tall with nodding racemes of white blooms.

Monarda species and cultivars
beebalm
2'–3' tall
Scarlet, white, pink blooms; fragrant leaves
Flowers summer
Sun
Zones 4–8
Use in border, butterfly, and hummingbird gardens

Native to North America. Intriguing flower form. Frequented by hummingbirds and butterflies. Susceptible to powdery mildew; 'Violet Queen' is more resistant than some others. Dwarf form, 'Petite Delight', grows to only 15 inches tall.

Nepeta x *faassenii*
catmint
18"–24" tall
Fragrant pale lavender, white blooms
Flowers summer
Sun to light shade
Zones 3–9
Use in border, butterfly, and container gardens,
    and as a groundcover

Soft, silver-gray leaves. Spreads readily. 'Six Hills Giant' has deeper violet flowers; 'Snowflake' has white blooms. Flowers are sterile; propagate by division. Cats love it!

Opuntia species
prickly pear (cholla)
6"–96" tall
Yellow, orange, red, pink, purple blooms
Flowers late spring to early summer
Sun
Zones 3–11
Use in border, container, and Xeriscape gardens

Native to North America. The hardiest include plains prickly pear, *O. polyacantha* (to Zone 3); hardy prickly pear, *O. compressa (humifusa)*, to Zone 4; and walking-stick cactus, *O. imbricata* (to Zone 6). Need well-drained soil. Combines well with grasses, succulents, and conifers.

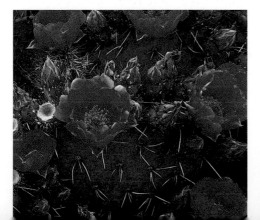

Oenothera fruticosa
sundrops
18"–24" tall
Bright yellow blooms
Flowers early summer
Sun
Zones 4–9
Use in border and naturalistic gardens,
    and as a groundcover

Native to North America. Blooms during the day, unlike fragrant evening primrose (*O. macrocarpa [missouriensis]*). Attractive red-tinged, evergreen leaf rosettes. Spreads quickly; control by pulling up unwanted plants.

Paeonia lactiflora cultivars
peony
18"–36" tall
Fragrant pink, white, red, and bicolor blooms
Flowers late spring to early summer
Full to partial sun
Zones 3–8
Use in border and cutting gardens

Single, anemone, semidouble, and double-flowered forms. Early, midseason, and late-blooming cultivars. Foliage makes attractive backdrop for later-blooming perennials. Very long-lived. Support plant with wire hoops. Cut stems to ground in fall; discard. Scores of cultivars; select by color and season of bloom.

Omphaloides cappadocica
omphaloides (navelwort)
6"–9" tall
Blue–and–white blooms
Flowers mid- to late spring
Light shade to shade
Zones 5–8
Use in naturalistic gardens and as a groundcover

Related to forget-me-nots. Sprays of bicolored flowers are lovely against the dark green foliage. Spreads slowly to about 18 inches. Prefers moist, well-drained soil. Easy to grow.

Paeonia suffruticosa cultivars
tree peony
3'–6' tall
Fragrant white, carmine, purple, yellow, pink
    blooms
Flowers late spring
Sun
Zones 6–8
Use in border gardens and as a specimen

Long-lived. Needs rich, moist, well-drained soil. Plant where it has shelter from harsh winds; protect from rabbits the first year with wire cage. Large flowers; remove them as soon as they fade to deter botrytis fungus.

Papaver orientale cultivars
oriental poppy
3'–4' tall
Pink, salmon, raspberry, red, white blooms,
   often splotched black-purple at base
Flowers late spring to early summer
Sun
Zones 3–8
Use in border, container, and cutting gardens

One of the showiest flowers for the border.
Easy care; will grow in almost any well-
drained soil. Leaves disappear by midsummer.

Pediocactus simpsonii var. *minor*
hedgehog cactus
2"–8" tall
Pink, magenta, white, yellow blooms
Flowers late spring to summer
Sun
Zones 6-11
Use in border, container, and Xeriscape gardens

Native to North America. Most are difficult to
grow on their own roots. This species is easy
to raise from seed, cuttings, or a graft. Grows
2½ inches tall, may form clumps, survives
cold winters best with a covering of snow.

Penstemon species and cultivars
beard-tongue (penstemon)
2'–4' tall
Red, pink, lavender, blue, white blooms
Flowers early to late summer
Sun
Zones 3–10, depending on species
Use in border, hummingbird, naturalistic, and
   Xeriscape gardens

Native to North America. Short-lived; finicky
about adapting outside its natural environment.
Needs excellent drainage. Susceptible to crown
rot; mulch with gravel, not organic material.
Most reseed freely.

perennial plants

Perovskia atriplicifolia
russian sage
3'–5' tall
Lavender, blue blooms; aromatic foliage
Flowers late summer to fall
Sun
Zones 5–9
Use in border and butterfly gardens

Silvery gray hairs cover the stems and
lanceolate or dissected leaves. Might get floppy
late in the season but remains attractive. Easy
to grow in well-drained soil. Provide winter
mulch in cold zones; cut back hard in spring.
Basically pest- and disease-free.

Phlox divaricata
wild sweet william
8"–12" tall
Blue, white blooms; slightly fragrant
Flowers midspring
Partial sun to light shade
Zones 3–9
Use in border and naturalistic gardens, and as
   a groundcover

Spreads slowly; never invasive. 'Fuller's White'
has white blooms; var. *laphamii* has deep
purple-blue flowers. Combines well with
bleeding heart and naturalized spring-
flowering bulbs. Evergreen in the South.
Prefers well-drained soil.

Phlox paniculata cultivars
garden phlox (summer phlox)
2'–4' tall
Fragrant pink, lavender, white, red blooms,
   often with deeper colored eye
Flowers mid- to late summer
Sun to light shade
Zones 4–9
Use in border, butterfly, and cutting gardens

Backbone of the perennial garden. Prefers rich,
well-drained soil; heavy feeder. Cut off spent
blooms for continuous flowering. Prone to
powdery mildew; do not water overhead. Select
resistant cultivars: lavender-blue 'Chattahoochee',
lavender 'Katherine', and white 'David'.

Phlox subulata
moss phlox (mountain pink)
4"–6" tall
Pink, white, blue, lavender, red blooms
Flowers midspring
Sun
Zones 2–9
Use in border and rock gardens, and as a
    groundcover

Foliage is semievergreen in the North, evergreen
in the South. Combines well with spring-
flowering bulbs. Prefers sandy, well-drained
soil. Shear after flowering. 'Red Wings', 'White
Delight', and 'Blue Hills' are good cultivars.

Polygonatum species and cultivars
solomon's seal
1'–3' tall
Greenish white blooms
Flowers late spring
Light shade
Zones 4–8
Use in naturalistic and woodland gardens

Native to North America. Easy care; needs
moist soil. Related European *P. odoratum*
'Variegatum' has fragrant flowers, which attract
hummingbirds, and cream-edged leaves.

Platycodon grandiflorus
balloon flower
18"–36" tall
Blue, white, pink blooms
Flowers early summer to fall
Sun to light shade
Zones 3–8
Use in border and cutting gardens

Intriguing, puffy buds like little balloons open
to star-shape blooms, which keep appearing if
you cut off spent blooms. Needs staking.
Long-lived perennial. Slow to break dormancy
in spring, so mark where you plant it.
Cultivars: white 'Albus', Shell Pink', 'Mariesii'.

Primula species and cultivars
primrose
6"–18" tall
Pink, white, blue, crimson, and bicolor blooms
Flowers early spring to early summer
Partial sun to light shade
Zones 5–9
Use in border, container, rock, and
    naturalistic gardens, and as a groundcover

Charming plants to light up shady spots.
Scores of cultivars, colors, and forms from
simple clusters to candelabra types. Needs
moist, acidic soil. Very pest-prone.

Polemonium caeruleum
jacob's ladder (greek valerian)
1'–2' tall
Blue blooms
Flowers late spring
Light shade to sun
Zones 3–9
Use in border and naturalistic gardens

Prefers moist, well-drained soil. Foliage,
arranged in rung-like fashion along the stems,
adds texture to the border or woodland.
Susceptible to mildew. There are white 'Album'
and variegated cultivars.

Pulmonaria species and cultivars
pulmonaria (lungwort)
8"–12" tall
Deep rose, coral red, blue, white blooms
Flowers spring
Light to full shade
Zones 3–9
Use in border and naturalistic gardens, and as
    a groundcover

Spreads quickly in moist soil. Easy to grow;
slugs may be a problem. Foliage is attractive all
season. *P. officinalis, P. longifolia,* and *P. saccharata*
have white-spotted leaves. Many cultivars.

121

Ranunculus acris
meadow buttercup
12"–15" tall
Bright yellow blooms
Flowers late spring to summer
Sun
Zones 5–8
Use in naturalistic gardens and as a groundcover

Easy to grow in any well-drained soil; reseeds with abandon. A favorite of children. 'Flore Pleno' is a double-flowered form, *Ranunculus repens* 'Buttered Popcorn' has finely dissected foliage edged in silvery green (zones 4–9).

Ratibida columnifera
prairie coneflower (mexican hat)
1'-2' tall
Yellow, brownish red blooms
Flowers summer
Sun
Zones 3-9
Use in border, bird, butterfly, cutting, and naturalistic gardens

Native to North America. Short-lived but reseeds. Not fussy but needs well-drained soil. Very finely dissected leaves. Combines well with ornamental grasses.

Rudbeckia species and cultivars
black–eyed susan
2'-3' tall
Yellow, bronze blooms
Flowers midsummer to fall
Sun
Zones 3-9
Use in border, butterfly, cutting, and naturalistic gardens

Native to North America. Easy to grow; long-lasting flowers; not fussy about soil or moisture. Not long-lived; reseeds prolifically. *R fulgida* blooms in July; 'Goldsturm' is a reliable 2-foot-tall cultivar. Combines with most perennials.

perennial plants

Salvia species and cultivars
salvia (sage)
1'-5' tall
Fragrant pink, white, lavender, blue, red blooms
Flowers early to late summer
Full sun to light shade
Zones 4-9
Use in border, butterfly, container, cutting, edible, naturalistic, and Xeriscape gardens

Sage for cooking; salvias for ornamentation. Attractive green, grayish, or variegated foliage and spikes of flowers. Undemanding and easy to grow. Many are native to North America. Some, such as culinary sage, are woody; cut back in spring before new growth begins.

Santolina chamaecyparissus
lavender cotton
18"-26" tall
Yellow blooms; fragrant foliage
Flowers early summer
Sun
Zones 6-10
Use in border and Xeriscape gardens

Grow this plant for its gray, divided foliage, not for the flowers. Makes an attractive low, clipped hedge around beds. Needs well-drained soil. Protect with a winter mulch in cool zones. Cut back plants in spring. 'Lambrook Silver' has silver foliage; 'Plumosus' has very lacy, silver foliage. *S. rosmarinifolia* is a green-leaved species.

Saponaria ocymoides (S. officinalis)
soapwort (bouncing bet)
4"-8" tall
Pink, red, white blooms
Flowers summer
Sun
Zones 3-8
Use in border and rock gardens

Mat-forming. Flower clusters practically cover the foliage; shear after flowering to keep it compact. Easy to grow in any soil. Cultivars include the tiny 'Bressingham', which grows to only 1 inch tall, and 'Rosea', with rose-colored flowers. Attractive along a path.

Saxifraga species and cultivars
saxifrage
3"–6" tall
Pink, carmine, white, yellow blooms; some fragrant
Flowers early to late summer
Light shade
Zones 3–8
Use in border and rock gardens, and as a
    groundcover

Clump-forming. Many have grayish green
leaves; leaves of *S. stolonifera* (strawberry
geranium) are white-veined above, red below.
Likes moist soil; dislikes hot summers.

Solidago species and cultivars
goldenrod
1'–3' tall
Yellow blooms
Flowers late summer to fall
Sun to light shade
Zones 3–10
Use in border, butterfly, cutting, and native gardens

Native to North America. Cultivars are more
garden-worthy and less invasive than species:
'Crown of Rays', 'Goldenmosa', dwarf 'Golden
Thumb'. Easy to grow in average soil.

Sedum species and cultivars
sedum
6"–24" tall
Pink, red, white, yellow, orange blooms
Flowers late spring to fall
Sun
Zones 3–9
Use in border, butterfly, container, Xeriscape,
    and rock gardens, and as a groundcover

Foliage is attractive all season. Clump-forming
or creeping. Easy to grow. Deep red seedpods
follow yellow blooms on *S. kamtschaticum*. The
trailing stems of *S. spurium* 'Dragon's Blood'
root where they touch soil. Pink flowers of
S. spectabile (now *Hylotelephium*) 'Autumn Joy' and
'Vera Jameson' deepen to rusty rose by fall.

Stachys byzantina
lamb's ears
12"–18" tall
Pinkish purple, mauve, magenta blooms
Flowers late spring to summer
Sun
Zones 5–8
Use in border gardens

Grown for its silvery, velvety foliage; the
cultivar 'Silver Carpet' does not produce
flowers. Easy to grow except in hot, humid
climates. *S. officinalis* (betony) has green,
crinkled foliage and reddish purple flower
spikes. Reseeds freely.

Sidalcea malviflora
checkerbloom
(miniature hollyhock)
2'–4' tall
Pink, white, red, purple blooms
Flowers mid- to late summer
Sun to light shade
Zones 5–9
Use in border, container, and cutting gardens

Native to North America. Easy to grow. Needs
well-drained soil. Seldom needs staking. Cut
back after first flowering to promote rebloom.
'Elsie Heugh' has fringed, light pink blooms;
'Scarlet Beauty' has deep purple flowers.

Stokesia laevis
stokes' aster
1'–2' tall
Blue, white, pink, and pale yellow blooms
Flowers late summer
Sun to light shade
Zones 5–10
Use in border, butterfly, and Xeriscape gardens

Native to North America. Evergreen in the
South. Long-flowering and easy to grow
almost anywhere. Needs well-drained soil.
Withstands heat and drought. Protect with
mulch in winter in cold zones.

Tanacetum parthenium
feverfew
12"–30" tall
White blooms with yellow centers
Flowers summer
Sun to light shade
Zones 5–9
Use in border, cutting, and naturalistic gardens

Easy to grow but not reliably hardy; self-seeds freely. Cut back after first flowering for rebloom in late summer. Foliage is aromatic. There are double- and yellow-flowered and yellow-leaved ('Aureum') forms.

Thalictrum species and cultivars
meadow rue
3'–5' tall
Pink, purple, lavender, yellow, and white blooms
Flowers early to late summer
Sun to light shade
Zones 5–8
Use in border, container, and naturalistic gardens

Graceful plant for rear of border or woodland planting. Blue-green leaves resemble those of columbine. Easy to grow, long-lived; prefers moist, well-drained soil. Flowers have sepals and prominent stamens, no petals. *T. flavum* ssp. *glaucum* is the most heat tolerant (Zone 9).

Thermopsis villosa
carolina lupine
3'–5' tall
Yellow blooms
Flowers early to midsummer
Sun to light shade
Zones 3–9
Use in border and naturalistic gardens

Native to North America. Attractive, divided foliage all season. Long-lived. Good specimen or rear-border plant. Combines well with ornamental grasses, wildflowers. May need staking if grown in rich soil or light shade.

perennial plants

Thymus species and cultivars
thyme
1"–12" tall
Fragrant lilac, crimson, pink, white blooms
Flowers in early summer
Sun
Zones 5–9
Use in border, container, edible, and rock gardens, and as a groundcover

So many to choose from; all easy to grow. Keep soil on dry side; cut back in spring. Gray-green or variegated leaves. Creeping thyme, *Thymus serpyllum*; lemon-scented, *T.* × *citriodorus*; silver, *T. vulgaris* 'Argenteus'; woolly, *T. pseudolanuginosus* (blooms insignificant).

Tiarella cordifolia
foamflower
6"–12" tall
White, pink, rose, maroon blooms
Flowers late spring
Sun to light shade
Zones 3–8
Use in border and woodland gardens, and as a groundcover

North American native. Pair with early spring bulbs, columbines, and ferns. Dislikes hot, dry climates; likes moist, acidic soil. 'Major', salmon pink blooms; 'Marmorata', purple-flecked leaves, maroon flowers; 'Purpurea', bronze-purple foliage, rose flowers. Spreads by underground runners.

Tradescantia virginiana
spiderwort
18"–30" tall
Blue, red, purple, magenta, pink, white blooms
Flowers late spring to summer
Sun to light shade
Zones 4–9
Use in border, container, and naturalistic gardens

Long-lived perennial. Easy to grow; not fussy about soil. Reseeds prolifically. Might rebloom in fall if entire plant is cut back when leaves begin to yellow. There are many cultivars, including 'Zwanenburg Blue', with intensely blue flowers; 'Rubra', deep rosy pink; 'Snowcap', white; and 'Congesta', purple.

Tricyrtis species and cultivars
toad lily
1'–3' tall
White, lilac, purple-spotted blooms
Flowers fall
Light shade to shade
Zones 5–9
Use in border and woodland gardens

Unusual plant with orchidlike blooms. Lovely by a path; combines well with hellebores, hostas, and ferns. Needs moist, slightly acidic soil. *T. formosana* 'Amethystina' has clusters of amethyst blue flowers; *T. hirta* 'Miyazaki', white blooms spotted lilac along arching stems.

Verbena species and cultivars
vervain
6"–48" tall
Purple, pink, and white blooms
Flowers summer to early fall
Sun
Zones 3–10
Use in border, container, and Xeriscape gardens

Very tolerant of drought and heat. Often reseeds freely. Rose verbena, *V. canadensis*, is often grown as an annual. Blue vervain, *V. hastata*, is long-blooming. *V. rigida* 'Alba' has white flowers. *V. bonariensis* is hardy to Zone 7.

Trillium species and cultivars
wake–robin (trillium)
1'–1½' tall
Pink, white, maroon, and yellow blooms
Flowers mid- to late spring
Light shade
Zones 3–8
Use in naturalistic and woodland gardens

Native to North America. Never collect from the wild; buy plants only from nurseries that can confirm that the plants are nursery-propagated (not just nursery-grown). Grows best where there is winter snowcover and on the West Coast. Prefers moist, well-drained soil. Combines well with bleeding hearts, primroses, epimedium, and ferns.

Veronica species and cultivars
speedwell (veronica)
1'–2' tall
Fragrant pink, rose, white, blue blooms
Flowers summer
Sun
Zones 4–8
Use in border and container gardens

Easy to grow. If soil is too rich, stems may sprawl and need staking. Cut back spent flowering stems to promote rebloom. Popular cultivars include pink 'Minuet', deep violet-blue 'Sunny Border Blue', true blue 'Crater Lake Blue', and 'White Icicle'.

Verbascum species and cultivars
mullein
2'–3' tall
Pale to sunny yellow blooms
Flowers early to late summer
Sun
Zones 4–8
Use in border and naturalistic gardens

Many mulleins are biennial, which produce large flower spikes in the second year. The perennials are not long-lived but do reseed. Needs well-drained soil. There are also white, pink, and purple species and hybrids.

Vinca minor
periwinkle (creeping myrtle)
2"–12" tall
Blue, white blooms
Flowers midspring
Sun to shade
Zones 4–9
Use as a groundcover

Evergreen. Spreads rapidly but not invasively by rooting along the stems. Easy to grow. Combines well with spring bulbs. 'Alba' has white flowers; 'Ralph Shugert', white-edged leaves; 'Flore Pleno', double-flowered blue.

shade-garden stars

Whether you look for a groundcover, a delicate backdrop for spring-blooming perennials and bulbs, or an easy-care filler, consider ferns. Although ferns are usually associated with shady, woodland areas where they are indispensable, many ferns will also grow well in gardens that receive dappled sunlight or a small amount of direct sun in the early morning or late afternoon, but not at midday (too hot and burning).

design considerations

Combine with broad-leaved plants, such as hellebores, hostas, and wild ginger, to accentuate the delicate appearance of feathery ferns. Taller ferns, such as ostrich and cinnamon, look good interplanted with evergreen shrubs.

Tall or short ferns combine well with spring-flowering bulbs. The fronds will camouflage the dying, yellowing foliage of the bulbs. Ferns add a lovely airy aspect to a garden. They are ideal fillers, as well.

cultural factors

The majority of ferns prefer moist, rich soil, but a few will grow on drier ground. Do not plant them too deep: Set the crowns at or just below ground level and cover with thin layer of soil. Mulch the area well to keep mud off the fronds and to conserve soil moisture.

While a fern is getting established in your garden, keep the soil constantly moist. If you plant ferns in sun or in warm zones, provide extra water through the growing season.

Adiantum pedatum
maidenhair fern
Deciduous
1'–2' tall
Shade to partial sun
Zones 3–8
Use in border, container, and naturalistic gardens, and as a groundcover

This is a tough, hardy plant, despite its delicate appearance, with pale green fronds on wiry stems. The fronds of southern maidenhair, *Adiantum capillus-veneris* (hardy only to Zone 8), emerge bronze-pink in spring and turn pale green as they mature. Needs constantly moist, lime-enriched soil.

Athyrium nipponicum 'Pictum'
japanese painted fern
Deciduous
12"–18" tall
Light shade to shade
Zones 3–8
Use in border and woodland gardens, and as a groundcover

Tricolored fronds make this one of the most beautiful ferns. Old fronds make a good mulch, so don't bother to remove them. Needs constantly moist, well-drained soil. Combines well with purple-leaved plants, such as 'Palace Purple' coralbells, and blue-leaved hostas.

fabulous ferns

Cyrtomium falcatum
holly fern
Evergreen
2'–3' tall
Partial sun to shade
Zones 6–10
Use in container and woodland gardens

Plants (native to Hawaii) grow well in containers, which you can bring indoors for winter in cold zones. Leaflets resemble leaves of English holly. Do not bury the crown when you plant. Site it in a sheltered spot. The related *Cyrtomium fortunei* (also called holly fern) is also hardy to Zone 6; it needs very well-drained soil to forestall rot in winter.

Dennstaedtia punctilobula
hay-scented fern
Deciduous
24"–30" tall
Shade to sun
Zones 3–9
Use in naturalistic gardens, and as a groundcover

Fronds smell like new-mown hay when crushed. Easy to grow, it tolerates wet or dry soil, sun or shade. Spreads fast; not recommended for small gardens. Excellent as a groundcover on a slope.

Dryopteris cristata
crested wood fern

Semievergreen
12"–30" tall
Light shade to shade
Zones 4–8
Use in border and woodland gardens

Fertile fronds stand erect and are taller than the sterile fronds. Prefers wet soil but will adapt to regular garden conditions if the soil is kept very moist. *D. clintoniana*, which may be a hybrid of *D. cristata* and *D. goldiana* (Goldie's wood fern), has broader, taller fronds.

Osmunda cinnamomea
cinnamon fern

Deciduous
2'–5' tall
Light shade to shade
Zones 3–8
Use in woodland gardens, and as a
    groundcover

Can be invasive but easy to pull up as it emerges in spring; spreads by underground runners. Fertile fronds are erect and dark brown. Sterile fronds form a shuttlecocklike rosette. Adaptable to sunny sites if provided with ample moisture.

Matteuccia struthiopteris
ostrich fern

Deciduous
3'–5' tall
Shade to sun
Zones 3–8
Use in woodland and naturalistic gardens,
    and as a groundcover; edible

Small, fertile fronds turn cinnamon brown as they mature. Loves wet, swampy soil but will grow in drier areas. Very hardy plant and easy to grow. Spreads slowly. You can collect the new spring fronds (the fiddleheads) to eat boiled or raw in salads.

Polystichum acrostichoides
christmas fern

Evergreen
18"–24" tall
Shade to partial sun
Zones 3–8
Use in cutting and woodland gardens, and as
    a groundcover

Native to North America. Fiddleheads are silvery haired as they emerge. Adaptable and easy to grow. Can tolerate more sun than most ferns, provided it has sufficient moisture. Appropriately named, it is long-lasting when cut for use indoors.

You can remove dead fronds in late fall, although they will decompose on their own, adding humus to the soil. In cold-winter climates, mulch the planting area as protection against the alternate freezing and thawing of the ground.

other attractive ferns

In addition to the ferns shown here, you may want to consider these:

lady fern, *Athyrium filix-femina,* has finely divided fronds. It is delicate in appearance but not in reality. Tolerant of sun, it makes an excellent groundcover in constantly moist soils in zones 3–8.

japanese sword fern, *Dryopteris erythrosora,* is evergreen. Its fronds are rosy brown when they emerge; they become rich green as they mature. It is hardy to Zone 5 (to Zone 4 with a winter mulch for protection).

sword fern, *Nephrolepis exaltata,* is a familiar houseplant and also an outdoor groundcover in shade or partial sun in mild climates (zones 9–11). Its large, 5-foot fronds are evergreen.

soft shield fern, *Polystichum setiferum,* has narrow fronds that lie close to the ground. Like lady fern, it appears delicate, but it is quite hardy and is tolerant of dry, poor soils. Hardy to Zone 5.

tassel fern, *Polystichum polyblepharum,* is evergreen with stiff fronds. It needs light to full shade and constant moisture. It grows in a vase shape to about 2 feet. Hardy in Zones 4–9.

cultivating beauties

Ornamental grasses prefer well-drained soil. With a few exceptions, they are drought- and heat-tolerant.

To take advantage of the extended seasons of interest of ornamental grasses, wait until spring to cut back leaves and flower stalks. The fluffy plumes remain attractive through winter, and the seeds often provide food for birds. Tall ornamental grasses look beautiful planted where early morning or late afternoon sun will shine through the foliage and plumes.

Note that many grasses that are tame garden subjects in colder zones can become aggressively invasive in mild climates, such as those of California and Florida.

Calamagrostis acutiflora 'Stricta'
feather reed grass
6'–7' tall
Green tinged reddish bronze to buff plumes
Flowers early summer
Sun to partial sun
Zones 5–9
Use in border and cutting gardens; as a specimen

Very showy, cool-climate grass. Tolerates wet or dry conditions and poor soil. Seed heads ripen from gold to silver through summer and fall. 'Karl Foerster' is shorter, 5 to 6 feet, and blooms slightly earlier.

Carex stricta 'Bowles Golden'
bowles golden sedge
2' tall
Creamy silver plumes
Flowers late spring
Sun to light shade
Zones 5–9
Use in border gardens, and as a specimen plant

Sedges (there are more than 1,000 species and cultivars) are grasslike perennials. Most often grown near or in water; must be constantly wet to thrive. Most will grow in light shade, where they combine well with ferns and hostas.

ornamental grasses

Cortaderia selloana
pampas grass
6'–9' tall
Silver-white leaves, plumes tinged red or purple
Flowers midsummer to early winter
Sun to light shade
Zones 7–10
Use in cutting gardens, and as a specimen plant

A stately, architectural plant. The razor-sharp leaves are evergreen in mild climates. Prefers moist soil. 'Gold Band' has yellow-edged leaves. Compact, dwarf 'Pumila' grows 4 to 6 feet tall, appropriate for a border. It can be invasive.

Festuca glauca
blue fescue
6"–18" tall
Blue-green foliage
Flowers summer
Sun
Zones 4–9
Use in border, container, and rock gardens

Lovely, tufted plant with steel blue leaves that last well into winter. Remove flowers, if you want, to concentrate attention on the foliage. Prefers dry, well-drained soil. Suffers in hot summer weather but recovers when temperatures cool. 'Elijah Blue' grows to 8 inches, with soft blue foliage; 'Glauca Minima' has intensely blue leaves.

Hakonechloa macra
hakone grass
1'–1½' tall
Reddish pink plumes
Flowers late summer to fall
Partial sun to light shade
Zones 5–9
Use in border and container gardens, and as a groundcover

Green, weeping foliage, reminiscent of bamboo; turns pinkish red in fall. Spreads slowly. Brightens shade gardens. 'Aureola' (shown) produces yellow leaves striped with narrow green lines; foliage burns in full sun, less yellow in deep shade.

Helictotrichon sempervirens
blue oat grass
1½'-2' tall
Straw-colored marked purple plumes
Flowers late spring to summer
Sun to partial sun
Zones 5–9
Use in border, container, and rock gardens

Rigid, steel blue or blue-green foliage. Attractive, small grass; like blue fescue but larger. Evergreen in warm climates. Does not like heavy, clay soils. Combines well with blue-leaved shrubs or contrasting perennials.

Panicum virgatum
switch grass
6'-7' tall
Pink, red, silver plumes
Flowers summer to fall
Sun to light shade
Zones 5–9
Use in cutting and naturalistic gardens, and as a specimen

North American tallgrass prairie native. Tolerates range of soils, climates, and moisture. Leaves turn yellow in fall. Forms tight, vertical clumps. 'Heavy Metal has pale metallic blue leaves.

Imperata cylindrica 'Red Baron' ('Rubra')
japanese blood grass
12"–18" tall
None
Sun to light shade
Zones 5–10
Use in border and container gardens, and as a specimen

This variety is grown for bright, wine red foliage, which becomes scarlet by fall. Effective when backlit by the setting sun. If a plant reverts to all-green, remove it immediately. (The green-leaved species spreads aggressively. A noxious weed, it cannot be sold in this country.

Pennisetum alopecuroides
fountain grass
3'-4' tall
Pink, white, and rose plumes
Flowers summer
Sun to light shade
Zones 6–9
Use in border, container, and cutting gardens

One of the most popular grasses for the middle and rear of a border. Plumes on laxly arching stems. Easy to grow; somewhat drought-tolerant. Dwarf 'Hameln' grows 1½ to 2 feet tall; does not grow well south of Zone 8. Very dwarf 'Little Bunny', only 12 inches tall, is a good rock-garden plant.

Miscanthus sinsensis 'Zebrinus'
zebra grass
5'-6' tall
Silver, tan plumes
Flowers summer
Sun
Zones 6–9
Use in border and bird gardens, and as a specimen

Very popular and easy to grow. Will grow near or in ponds. Leaves of 'Zebrinus' and 'Strictus' (porcupine grass) have horizontal bands of yellow. 'Gracillimus' has showy flowers. 'Purpurascens' has orange-red fall color.

Pleioblastus species
bamboo
18"–72" tall
No flowers; grown for handsome leaves
Sun to light shade
Zones 6–9
Use in Oriental-style gardens, and as a specimen and screen plant

Stems (culms) are hollow. Peaceful rustling when it moves in a breeze. Contain bamboo with concrete edging at least 2 feet deep if it is a running, not clumping, species. Pygmy bamboo, *P. pygmaeus*, and dwarf white-striped bamboo, *P. variegatus*, are good garden choices.

designing with rainbow plants

Iris are aptly named for the goddess of the rainbow. They have flowers in every hue, including a wide range of blues. You will want them in your garden, though, for more reasons than that. They are easy to grow, bloom from early spring to summer (depending on the varieties you choose), and are just as beautiful in a vase indoors as they are in the garden. They are, however, much longer lasting in the garden.

Although there are some iris that reflower in fall, most do not rebloom. Their leaves, however, are attractive vertical accents for months. Plant iris in a border with almost any other perennial that has similar or contrasting growth habits: daylilies, peonies, dianthus, columbines, ferns, cranesbills, hostas, and primroses. Hostas are particularly effective with iris that have variegated leaves.

a bit of definition

Falls: The outer, usually drooping row of petal-like sepals, often a darker color than the rest of the flower.

Standards: The inner row of petals, which may lie horizontally across the falls or stand upright.

Beard: A fuzzy tuft emerging from the blossom throat and continuing down the falls. It is usually a different color, often yellow, than the petals.

Signal: Markings of contrasting color at the base of the falls; they attract insects, such as bees, and show them the way in to the pollen. Veins along the petals and beards provide the same guidance.

Self: A flower with falls and standards of the same color.

Iris cristata
crested iris
6"–12" tall
Lavender-blue, purple, white blooms
Flowers midspring
Sun to light shade
Zones 6–9
Use in border, container and naturalistic
    gardens, and as a groundcover

Native to North America. The earliest iris to bloom. Exquisite plant. Spreads slowly. Provide extra water in sunny gardens. 'Alba' has white flowers.

iris

Iris × *germanica*
bearded iris (german iris)
18" tall
Fragrant deep and pale violet blooms
Flowers late spring
Sun
Zones 3–10
Use in border and cutting gardens

One of the parents of modern bearded iris. Its origin is unknown; it might actually be a natural hybrid. The flowers are quite large. Easy to grow. Tolerant of many soil and climate conditions. *I.* × *germanica* var. *florentina* has very pale blue standards.

Iris ensata (kaempferi) cultivars
japanese iris
2'–3' tall
Fragrant violet, blue, lavender, yellow,
    white blooms
Flowers early summer
Sun to light shade
Zones 6–9
Use in border, cutting, and water gardens

One of the last iris to bloom. Attractive near or in ponds and streams. Intolerant of limey soils. Scores of hybrids, many of which are tetraploids (extra chromosomes), which produce larger, longer-lasting flowers.

Iris hybrids
louisiana iris
2'–4' tall
Blue, pink, red, purple, yellow blooms
Flowers late spring to summer
Sun to light shade
Zones 4–9
Use in border and cutting gardens

Louisiana hybrids include several species native to southern North America and their natural and man-made hybrids. The beardless flowers are lovely. Plants are adaptable but prefer moist soil while in bloom. Tolerate heat and humidity; some go dormant in summer.

Iris pallida
orris (dalmation iris)
3'–4' tall
Fragrant lilac–blue, lavender blooms
Flowers late spring to early summer
Sun
Zones 4–9
Use in border gardens

The root is used as a fixative in perfumery and potpourri. A parent of the modern tall bearded iris. The silvery green leaves may be semievergreen. There are varieties with striped leaves: 'Variegata' (cream), 'Alba Variegata' (white), and 'Aurea Variegata' (yellow).

Iris sibirica
siberian iris
2'–3' tall
Blue, purple, magenta, pink, white, yellow
   blooms
Flowers late spring to early summer
Sun to light shade
Zones 3–9
Use in border and cutting gardens

Beardless. Grasslike leaves are attractive all summer. Easy to grow. Graceful flowers with hybrids in a wide range of colors and bicolors: white and yellow 'Butter and Sugar', red-purple 'Ruffled Velvet', deep blue self 'Swank'.

Iris pseudacorus
yellow flag
2½'–5' tall
Yellow, white blooms
Flowers early to midsummer
Sun to light shade
Zones 3–9
Use in border, cutting, and water gardens

A beardless iris at home near or in water. Reseeds freely. Adapts to garden conditions as long as you provide constant moisture. 'Alba' has creamy white blooms. The leaves of 'Variegata' start out yellow-striped and mature to green.

Iris versicolor
blue flag
2'–3' tall
Blue blooms, blotched yellow with purple veins
Flowers late spring to early summer
Sun to light shade
Zones 3–9
Use in border, cutting, and water gardens

Native to eastern North America. Prefers wet conditions; will adapt to garden conditions if constant moisture and humus-rich soil are provided. The rhizome is highly poisonous. Southern blue flag, *I. virginica*, grows to 2 feet.

cultural factors
Most iris prefer moist to wet soil and, especially in warm zones, some protection (shade) from midday sun. Plant bearded iris with the rhizome at the soil surface.

The best time to dig up and divide most iris is in fall. Most are so adaptable, however, that you can divide them anytime they are not in bloom, although midsummer would certainly reduce their chances for survival.

Remove yellowed, dead foliage in late fall and compost or discard it.

other beautiful iris
dwarf iris, *Iris verna*, has very fragrant, violet-blue flowers from mid- to late spring. Beardless, it is native to eastern North America. The foliage is evergreen in mild climates. Hardy in zones 6–9.

red iris, *I. fulva*, is a lovely native plant with rusty red flowers that are more open and flat-topped than other iris. It blooms in late spring and needs very moist soil. Hardy in zones 6–9.

gladwin iris, *I. foetidissima*, is also known as stinking iris, an appropriate name because the foliage is malodorous. The seeds are the reason for its inclusion in so many gardens. The seedpods open in autumn to reveal unusual and decorative, reddish orange seeds that persist through winter. The leaves are evergreen. Hardy in zones 5–9.

winter iris, *I. unguicularis*, starts to bloom in December in areas with very mild winters and continues through February. It has fragrant, violet-blue flowers, which are good for cutting, and evergreen foliage. Hardy in zones 8–10.

sources

Most nursery, home, and garden centers carry the supplies you will need. If you can't find what you're looking for, here are some resources:

American Horticulture Society (AHS)
7931 East Boulevard Dr.
Alexandria, VA 22308
703-768-5700
www.ahs.com
A good source for information about plant hardiness, new plant releases, and other horticultural information. Their website has an excellent list of gardening websites and other resources.

Perennial Plant Association (PPA)
3383 Schirtzinger Rd.
Hilliard, OH 43026
614-771-8431
www.perennialplant.org
A source for the latest information on how a specific plant performs in your region and where to acquire plants.

Mail-Order Nurseries

Burpee (free)
300 Park Ave.
Warminster, PA 18991-0001
800-888-1447
www.burpee.com

Forestfarm ($4)
990 Tetherow Rd.
Williams, OR 97544-9599
541-846-7269
www.forestfarm.com

Greer Gardens ($3)
1280 Goodpasture Island Rd.
Eugene, OR 97401
541-686-8266
www.greergardens.com

Heronswood Nursery Ltd. ($8)
7530 NE 288th St.
Kingston, WA 98346
360-297-4172
www.heronswood.com

Jackson & Perkins Co. (free)
2518 S. Pacific Hwy.
Medford, OR 97501
800-292-4769
www.jacksonandperkins.com

Kurt Bluemel, Inc. ($3)
2740 Greene Ln.
Baldwin, MD 21013-9523
800-248-7584
www.bluemel.com

Louisiana Nursery ($5)
5853 Highway 182
Opelousas, LA 70570
318-948-3696

Musser Forests (free)
P.O. Box S-91 M
Indiana, PA 15701
800-643-3819
www.musserforests.com

Niche Gardens ($3)
1111 Dawson Rd.
Chapel Hill, NC 27516
919-967-0078
www.nichegdn.com

Plant Delights Nursery (One box of
   chocolates or ten stamps)
9241 Sauls Rd.
Raleigh, NC 27603
919-772-4794
www.plantdelights.com

Roslyn Nursery ($2)
211 Burrs Ln.
Dix Hills, NY 11746
631-643-9347
www.roslynnursery.com

Thompson & Morgan, Inc. (free)
P.O. Box 1308
Jackson, NJ 08527-0308
800-274-7333
www.thompson-morgan.com

Tranquil Lake Nursery ($1)
45 River St.
Rehoboth, MA 02769-1395
800-353-4344
www.tranquil-lake.com

Van Bourgondien (free)
P.O. Box 1000
Babylon, NY 11702
800-622-9959
www.dutchbulbs.com

White Flower Farm (free)
P.O. Box 50
Litchfield, CT 06759-0050
800-503-9624
www.whiteflowerfarm.com

Woodlanders ($2)
1128 Colleton Ave.
Aiken, SC 29801
803-648-7522

Garden Supplies

Gardener's Supply Company
128 Intervale Rd.
Burlington, VT 05401
800-955-3370
www.gardeners.com

Kinsman Co.
River Rd.
Point Pleasant, PA 18950
803-733-4146
www.kinsmangarden.com

Lagenbach Tools
638 Lindero Canyon Rd., MSC 290
Oak Park, CA 91301-5464
800-362-1991
www.langenbach.com

Plants from the Internet

http://www.bhglive.com
http://www.garden.com
http://www.landscapeusa.com

index

Bowles golden sedge (*Carex stricta* 'Bowles Golden'), *32*, *40*, *53*, 102, 128, *128*

Boxwood, 41, 87

Brick path, *42*, *67*, 68–71, *68–71*, *70–71*

Brick wall, 62

Brunnera macrophylla, 102, 105, 109, *109*

Buckwheat, *48*

Buffalograss, 45

Bugbane, 19, 87

Bugleweed, 92

Bulbs, 14, 124, 126

Butterfly bush, *39*

Butterfly, 6, 36–37, *39*, 118

    garden, 36–39, *36–39*, 106, 108, 110, 111, 113–120, 122

    house, *39*

Butterfly weed (*Asclepias tuberosa*), 10, *39*, 102, 108, *108*

Cardoon, *67*

Carex stricta 'Bowles Golden', 102, 128, *128*

Carolina lupine (*Thermopsis villosa*), 102, 124, *124*

Catmint (*Nepeta × faassenii*), *36*, *46*, *66*, 102, 119, *119*

Catnip, *66*

Centaurea, 90

Centranthus ruber, 103, 104, 110, *110*

Cerastium tomentosum, 105, 110, *110*

Chamaemelum nobile, 102, 110, *110*

Chamomile (*Chamaemelum nobile*), *64*, 102, 110, *110*

Checkerbloom (*Sidalcea malviflora*), 79, 102, 123, *123*

Chelone

    glabra, 105, 110, *110*

    lyonii, 110

Chives (*Allium schoenoprasum*), *50*, *64*, *67*, 106

Chocolate mint, *79*

Cholla (*Opuntia* spp.), *48*, *50*, *51*, 102, 119, *119*

Christmas fern (*Polystichum acrostichoides*), 102, 127, *127*

Christmas rose, *56*, 115

Chrysanthemum, *43*, *79*, 93, 102, 111, *111*

Cinnamon fern (*Osmunda cinnamomea*), *29*, 102, 126, 127, *127*

Clematis, 9, *9*, *59*, 79, *81*, 102, 111, *111*

Climate zone, 15, 144, *144*

Climbing rose, *18*, 79, 111

Cocoa bean hulls, 85

Colewort (*Crambe cordifolia*), 8, *8*, *36*, 102, 111, *111*

Color, 6, 7, *7*, 22

Columbine, (*Aquilegia* spp.), 8, 10, 22, 23, *23*, 28, *58–59*, *80*, 102, 107, *107*, 124, 130

Compost, 84, 85

Coneflower, purple, 11, *11*, *33*, 38, *38*, 41, *42–43*, 104, 113, *113*

Container garden, 106–126, 128–130

Contemplative garden, 52–55, *52–55*

Convallaria majalis, 104, 111, *111*

Coralbells (*Heuchera* spp.), 28, 41, 43, 57, 87, 90, 102, 115, *115*

Coreopsis, 8, *8*, 23, *33*, 38, *46*, 87, *92*, 102, 107, 111, *111*

    'Moonbeam', 57

Cortaderia selloana, 104, 128, *128*

Corydalis, 8, 28, *29*, *68*, 102, 111, *111*

    lutea, 102, 111, *111*

Coryphantha spp., *51*

Cosmos, 20

Cottage-style garden, 6, 14–15, *14–15*, 95, 113

Crambe, 8, *8*, *36*, 102, 103, 111, *111*

    cordifolia, 102, 103, 111, *111*

Cranesbill (*Geranium* spp.), *18*, *45*, *47*, *72*, 102, 103, 114, *114*, 130

Crassula, *46*

Creeping juniper, 45

Creeping myrtle (*Vinca minor*), 103, 125, *125*

Creeping phlox, 8, 9, *9*

Crested iris (*Iris cristata*), 103, 130, *130*

Crested wood fern (*Dryopteris cristata*), 103, 127, *127*

Crocosmia cvs., 104, 112, *112*

Crocus, 49

Cushion spurge (*Euphorbia polychroma*), 103, 114, *114*

Cutting garden, 79, 106–124, 127–131

Cyclamen hederifolium, 103, 112, *112*

Cyrtomium falcatum, 103, 126, *126*

index

index

index

index

photography credits

Charles Mann:
8 (top right, bottom right),
105 (bottom left), 106 (top left),
107 (bottom right), 108 (top left,
top right), 109 (bottom center,
bottom right), 111 (bottom right),
112 (top left), 114 (top center),
117 (top left, bottom left),
122 (top center, top right),
123 (bottom center, top right),
124 (top right), 126 (bottom right)

Saba S. Tien:
24, 29 (bottom), 39 (top left, top right),
55 (bottom), 56–57, 58 (bottom),
59 (left, top right), 64–65,
66 (top, bottom right), 67 (left),
106 (bottom right), 108 (bottom right),
111 (top right), 116 (bottom center),
124 (bottom center), 126 (top center,
top right, bottom left)

acknowledgements
The gardens and gardeners:
David Clem & Ton Stam,
Rosalind Creasy, Rizz Arthur Dean,
Rosemary Kautzky, Kelly & Kelly
Nursery, Robert Kourick, Susan & Jay
Kuhlman, Preston Winery,
Lauren Springer, Saba S. Tien,
Willow Glen Nursery

metric conversions

U.S. Units to Metric Equivalents

to convert from	multiply by	to get
Inches	25.400	Millimetres
Inches	2.540	Centimetres
Feet	30.480	Centimetres
Feet	0.3048	Metres
Yards	0.9144	Metres
Square inches	6.4516	Square centimetres
Square feet	0.0929	Square metres
Square yards	0.8361	Square metres
Acres	0.4047	Hectares
Cubic inches	16.387	Cubic centimetres
Cubic feet	0.0283	Cubic metres
Cubic feet	28.316	Litres
Cubic yards	0.7646	Cubic metres
Cubic yards	764.550	Litres

Metric Units to U.S. Equivalents

to convert from	multiply by	to get
Millimetres	0.0394	Inches
Centimetres	0.3937	Inches
Centimetres	0.0328	Feet
Metres	3.2808	Feet
Metres	1.0936	Yards
Square centimetres	0.1550	Square inches
Square metres	10.764	Square feet
Square metres	1.1960	Square yards
Hectares	2.4711	Acres
Cubic centimetres	0.0610	Cubic inches
Cubic metres	35.315	Cubic feet
Litres	0.0353	Cubic feet
Cubic metres	1.308	Cubic yards
Litres	0.0013	Cubic yards

To convert from degrees Celsius (C) to degrees Fahrenheit (F), multiply by ⁹⁄₅; then add 32.

To convert from degrees Fahrenheit (F) to degrees Celsius (C), first subtract 32; then multiply by ⁵⁄₉.

zone map

range of average annual minimum temperatures for each zone

	Zone 1	Below -50°F
	Zone 2	-50° to -40°
	Zone 3	-40° to -30°
	Zone 4	-30° to -20°
	Zone 5	-20° to -10°
	Zone 6	-10° to 0°
	Zone 7	0° to 10°
	Zone 8	10° to 20°
	Zone 9	20° to 30°
	Zone 10	30° to 40°
	Zone 11	Above 40°